HOPE
AND
HEALING
FROM
EMOTIONAL
ABUSE

HOPE
AND
HEALING
FROM
EMOTIONAL
ABUSE

GREGORY L. JANTZ, PhD

with Ann McMurray

SPIRE

© 1995, 2003, 2009 by Gregory L. Jantz

Published by Revell
a division of Baker Publishing Group
P.O. Box 6287, Grand Rapids, MI 49516-6287
www.revellbooks.com

Spire edition published 2013

Previously published under the title *Healing the Scars of Emotional Abuse*

ISBN 978-0-8007-8831-5

Printed in the United States of America

Unless otherwise indicated, Scripture quotations are from the Holy Bible, New International Version®. NIV®. Copyright © 1973, 1978, 1984 by Biblica, Inc.™ Used by permission of Zondervan. All rights reserved worldwide. www.zondervan.com

Scripture marked NASB is taken from the New American Standard Bible®, Copyright © 1960, 1962, 1963, 1968, 1971, 1972, 1973, 1975, 1977, 1995 by The Lockman Foundation. Used by permission.

To protect the privacy of those involved, names have been changed in all of the case studies used in this book.

13   14   15   16   17   18   19   7   6   5   4   3   2   1

Contents

Contents

Part 1

UNDERSTANDING
EMOTIONAL ABUSE

1

What Is Emotional Abuse?

There is no scar tissue to stretch, no bruises to yellow and heal, no gaping wound to point to. In spite of their invisibility, emotional wounds comprise a very damaging form of abuse.

David was eighteen years old when he killed himself. He was never physically beaten or sexually molested by anyone, yet David was the victim of abuse. At the time no one put that name on it. His death was tragic, certainly, but no one ever stopped to think about his life. David died as a result of lifelong emotional abuse—continual, pervasive, easily denied and overlooked emotional abuse.

David's father had been a football player all through school. He had the same dream for his son. There was just one problem. He never stopped long enough in his pursuit of athletic excellence for his son to ask David if *he* wanted to be a football player. He just assumed David would want to excel in sports as he had.

As expected, David played football growing up. In fact, he did excel at it, being physically large and strong for his age. It was even fun at first—the roar of the crowd, the overwhelming attention lavished on him by his family, the obvious pride others took in his athletic ability. But the pressure to succeed, to live up to his father's expectations, was tremendous. As time went on, no matter how well David did, there was always another level to reach, more he still had to do. No longer was David competing against another team or against other children; instead, he was competing against his father's expectations of how much he himself had accomplished (or thought he had) at the same age.

Eventually the pressure got so intense David could no longer cope. When he was fifteen, he tried to kill himself. The attempt failed, but the injuries he suffered because of the attempt left him unable to compete in sports. David had ingested a common poison that settled into his joints, weakening them so that sports were now totally out of the question. Even though he was still alive, David thought he was off the hook. Maybe now his father would stop trying to force him to be a football player and would listen to what David really wanted to be—an artist.

The pressure to compete in sports did indeed stop, but so did everything else. David became the invisible person in the family. No longer the focus of his father's sports ambition, David found there was no other place for him in the family. David's sister, Janice, became the athlete of the family. Built strong, like David, she excelled in two sports: track and field and gymnastics. She lettered in both sports in high school and competed at the state level. David's role diminished steadily, outshined by the light of his sister's athletic accomplishments.

Completely convinced of his own worthlessness, David gradually lost all hope of ever recapturing his father's attention.

His exceptional artistic ability and vision were not valued in his family. Because of David's lack of performance, his birthright had been passed to his younger sister.

One spring day, during one of Janice's high school track meets, David escaped to his room. Determined to be successful this time, he put a bullet through his brain with a shotgun.

When news of his death became known, everyone agreed it was a terrible tragedy. But then they all remembered, shaking their heads, that he had tried it once before. He always had been a messed-up kid. David's inability to cope with life was attributed to some tragic defect in his personality. No one ever stopped to consider that David had been abused all his life. He had never been beaten or molested, but David died of abuse—emotional abuse. Leaving no marks, it still left him dead.

Unacknowledged Abuse

As a professional counselor treating eating disorders for almost twenty-five years, I am very concerned about the often overlooked issue of emotional abuse. For many years I have noticed that the focus of abuse, even the concept of abuse, has centered around the physical beatings, outward neglect, and sexual invasion of children. The signs of emotional abuse, however, are easier to overlook. There is no scar tissue to stretch, no bruises to yellow and heal, no gaping wound to point to. In spite of their invisibility, emotional wounds comprise a very damaging form of abuse.

While emotional abuse always accompanies physical and sexual abuse, it can also be present on its own. Because its implications have been overlooked, it has been left to do its damage in silence. The abused have no recourse but to wonder why they just can't seem to get their lives on track. Each will think back to his or her childhood and won't be able to come up with a single time that Dad backhanded him across the room, or Mom left her alone for days at a time with no food, or a cousin wanted to do "naughty" things behind the house when the adults weren't looking. These people conclude, therefore, that they were never abused and delve no further into their past to discover why their present doesn't seem to be working.

Emotional abuse is harder to spot and easier to deny. But just as physical and sexual abuse have signposts to mark their presence, emotional abuse, being a systematic attack on one's sense of self, has common traits. Just as physical and sexual abuse come in degrees of severity, emotional abuse runs the gamut of intensity and damage. It exists, apart from physical or sexual abuse, as incredibly destructive to an emerging sense of self.

All of us have, at one time or another, come under attack by people who just happen to be having a bad day. They take out their frustrations on us, and we feel battered by the winds of their emotions. We have all had it happen to us, and we have all probably been guilty of it a time or two. No one is perfect, and all of us slip up and occasionally say or do things we know we shouldn't. That's normal.

Emotional abuse isn't normal. Emotional abuse is the consistent pattern of being treated unfairly and unjustly over a period of time, usually by the same person or people. It can also be a onetime traumatic event that is left unresolved. Emotional abuse is an intentional assault by one person on another to so distort the victim's view of self that the victim allows the abuser to control him or her.

In some ways, emotional abuse is the most common form of abuse. It comes from the mother who yells in frustration every time her son makes a mistake, "Why can't you be more like your sister?" Or from the father who snorts in derision as he proclaims regularly to everyone who will listen, "This girl won't amount to *nothin'*!" It comes from the husband who tells his wife, "You're too stupid to get a job!" Over and over again, the pattern is repeated until the repetition obscures the severity. The son will think to himself, *Mom always says that—what's the big deal?* The daughter will be silent and decide, *It doesn't matter what you think!* The wife deep inside will agree, *I guess I'm not smart enough.* Each will attempt to minimize the damage in order to continue on with life as he or she knows it.

Like other forms of abuse, emotional abuse can be self-perpetuating, repeating the cycle throughout relationships and across generations. If emotional abuse occurs early in life, it can cause dysfunctional behavior into the adult years.

It is important to understand that abuse has a broad definition as well as broad effects. While physical and sexual abuse can be much more visible and therefore are considered more severe, it is vital not to measure abuse on a scale of "bad" to "worse." Rather, it is important to acknowledge its presence, whether in the past or the present. Emotional abuse always accompanies physical or sexual abuse but stands fully on its own as damaging and destructive to an individual.

So many of the people I have counseled over the years started out by telling me, "It's not like I was abused or anything. . . ." They then proceeded to recount horror stories of growing up with what I strongly believe is emotional abuse. Too often they seemed embarrassed as they talked, as if fearful of making "too big a deal" out of what had happened to them. Attempting to minimize their abuse is one of the chief denial techniques developed to survive emotionally through the abuse.

So how do you know if you have been abused in the past or if the relationship you are in now is an abusive one? Often you aren't the best judge. If you have grown up in an abusive family, your experiences will all have a bizarre sense of normalcy. If you compare your abusive past with a current abusive relationship and vice versa, there will appear to be nothing different to point to the reality of abuse.

However, even if you are not the *best* judge, you are really the *only* judge. In my counseling, I have found that when people suspect they were abused, in most cases they were. If the relationship you had in the past or the one you have now is with a person or people who consistently make you feel worthless, you are being abused. All of us need relationships with people who love us, who build us up, and who support us as we learn and grow.

Of course, not all relationships are perfect, and people say or do things in anger that they regret later. But if those things are a pattern, and if they are used to degrade and control, no matter how subtle they may seem or how much the other person tells you they are really for "your own good," in truth they are abuse. You may be asking yourself, "Where does constructive criticism end and abuse take over?" This book is designed to help you identify the signs and common types of emotional abuse and know what to do about it.

Emotional abuse by itself or used in conjunction with physical or sexual abuse is easily recognizable if you know what to look for. Many of the types of abuse identified in this book will take the form of a message—the spoken and unspoken messages passed on to you as a child that constitute the basic structure of your self-identity and self-esteem. These messages, either positive or negative, have become incorporated into how you feel about yourself. Whether you were emotionally abused as a child or an adult, the messages were meant to belittle, devalue, shame, and ultimately control. Additionally, if those messages were given by the very people you looked to for love and guidance, the very ones whose opinions you trusted, they have been given the appearance of validity and have added weight.

Just as this book will help you identify the abuse, it will also help you identify the abuser. Emotional abusers have very select ways they use to control those they are abusing. The messages may differ slightly, but the ultimate goal of emotional abuse is control. By controlling those around them, abusers are attempting to control their circumstances and situations. By belittling those around them, abusers are attempting to make themselves feel better.

The tragedy is that while sometimes these abusers are aware of what they are doing, often they are not. A habit of abuse has become a life pattern that is so comfortable, so normal for them, that they have stopped questioning the reasons behind their words and actions. As is so often the case in abuse, many abusers have a history of abuse in their own past and are acting out behavior that seems normal to them.

As you are reading this book, you may discover that you are perpetuating the pattern of emotionally abusive behaviors yourself. It is vitally important that you accept this truth and continue to work through the book to help bring awareness and hope. If you are emotionally abusive to those around you, now is the time to change your pattern. Be alert to the messages that are being identified as abusive and decide to change. Kindness, compassion, empathy, and affection may not have been characteristics you grew up observing, and therefore you did not have the chance to model them fully in your adult life. If you were raised in an abusive environment and realize you are perpetuating that environment, it is possible to intentionally alter the way you relate to yourself and others. The first step is knowledge—knowing how harmful your behaviors are to those you love, and to yourself, can provide you with the motivation to make positive changes.

Also, as you are reading this book, you may come face-to-face with a past or a present that is painful to remember or accept. The goal is not to injure you all over again by bringing up a hurtful past; rather, it is to help you understand the behavior and place it in the proper context of your life. The further goal is to motivate you to avoid repeating the behavior yourself, either through how you relate to others or how you relate to yourself.

Remember as you are reading this book that it is important to avoid trying to measure your abuse against some scale. Whether it is a long-term abusive relationship or a onetime traumatic event of rejection that created a later resentment and unresolved anger, it is still damaging. It is vital that you identify it and learn how to deal with its consequences. Acknowledging and becoming aware of abusive patterns in your life will lead to healing and the recovery process.

Understanding Emotional Abuse

Look over the following signs of emotional abuse and think about your childhood. Think also about any patterns that are familiar to you in your present relationships. Under "Past" mark those that you remember as being a consistent part of your childhood. Under "Present" mark those that are part of your current relationships. If you recognize an abusive behavior or message you are perpetuating in your own life, place your initial after it. Remember, this is not for anyone else to see. This is for you to use to begin to identify the presence of emotional abuse in your past and present.

Signs of Emotional Abuse	Past	Present
Making the person feel worthless	——	——
Putting the blame for one's mistakes on the other person	——	——
Minimizing the other person's point of view	——	——
Threatening or hinting of physical or sexual abuse	——	——
Going into fits of rage and anger	——	——
Failing to fulfill commitments or promises made or implied	——	——
Lying to avoid responsibility for the truth	——	——
Refusing to acknowledge the other person's feelings	——	——
Verbally or physically humiliating the other person through inappropriate gestures, comments, or "jokes"	——	——
Using shame or guilt to manipulate the actions of the other person	——	——
Not allowing the other person to articulate his or her feelings	——	——
Denying the person access to his or her personal possessions or pets	——	——
Withholding financial resources	——	——
Refusing to communicate with the other person—the silent treatment	——	——
Displaying extreme ranges of mood	——	——

Signs of Emotional Abuse	Past	Present
Making conditional agreements in which the conditions keep changing to avoid fulfilling the agreement	——	——
Using a hostile or sarcastic tone of voice with the other person	——	——
Being critical of each action, thought, or remark of the other person	——	——
Viewing others as a part of that person's own personality as opposed to individuals with their own thoughts, feelings, and opinions	——	——
Belittling, humiliating, marginalizing, and/or ignoring the other person	——	——

A Time to Heal

Think about this next statement. Take some time to respond to what it represents in your life—both past and present—if you have been abused or have abused: *Emotional abuse keeps you from understanding and envisioning the person you were created to be.*

1. If you could come up with one reason why you chose to read this book, what would it be?
2. How did you feel as you worked through the signs of emotional abuse? Were you able to mark down the signs, or did you find yourself hesitating and trying to explain away some of them?
3. If you were able to mark them down, do you see any patterns emerging between what you put in the past and what is happening in the present?
4. If you hesitated and tried to explain away some of the signs, why do you suppose that is?

5. As you completed marking the signs of emotional abuse, did you stop and count how many signs you identified? If you marked just a few, how does that make you feel? If you marked many, how does that make you feel?

6. As you look back over what you marked, are you able to identify the one or two signs that did the most damage to your sense of self? Why were these so damaging to you?

Going through the signs of emotional abuse isn't some sort of test. Whether you marked one sign or many, your experience is not meant to be judged against another. This exercise is merely a way for you to evaluate your experiences. It's also a way to validate that the conduct, thoughts, or actions described are wrong and harmful. If you have identified these signs in the behaviors of people you love, sometimes it's hard to accept the truth.

Accepting truth can be very difficult, especially when the truth involves pain. Yet in John 8:32, Jesus says that knowing the truth will set us free.

1. What truth have you had difficulty accepting as you think about your past? Your present?

2. In order to honor truth fully, go through the above exercise again and make sure you have honestly marked your past and present experience. Mark the three answers that are most significant to you at this time. These can be either past or present.

3. Perhaps one of the most known verses in Scripture is John 3:16. It says, "For God so loved the world that he gave his

one and only Son, that whoever believes in him shall not perish but have eternal life." Emotional abuse tells you you're not worthy to be loved. How do you reconcile that with what God has not only told you but done?

4. Is it easier for you to believe another person or God? Why?

5. First Peter 2:9 says that we are chosen, royalty, and holy in God's eyes and in his plans. How has emotional abuse kept you from understanding or envisioning the person God created you to be?

6. Following are three affirmation statements. Read them aloud:

- God sees me as a person of worth and great value, and he views others that way as well.

- With God's help, I can overcome a past of emotional abuse and find healing and wholeness as a person.

- With God's help, I can have the courage to set appropriate boundaries for how other people treat me and how I treat others.

You were created to have emotional freedom, inner peace, and strong self-esteem. Emotional abuse has undermined God's plan for your life, your joy, and your peace. But what others have sabotaged, God can rebuild. It begins with accepting the truth of emotional abuse—the damage it does and the role it has played and still plays in your life.

2

Why Is Emotional Abuse
So Common?

Like a constant ringing in the ears or background noise,
the frequency of emotional abuse has caused us to try to
ignore it since we can't ever seem to get away from it. And
if we can ignore it, we can deny not only its existence but
also its effects.

There's an often-told parable about a man who arrives at his
workplace to find his boss running around the office screaming because central dispatch called and complained about a
missed production schedule. The man gets chewed out by
his fuming boss all day for a variety of reasons. Upon finally
arriving home after being verbally beaten all day, he finds that
his wife has spent too much time shopping and dinner isn't
on the table yet. Erupting in anger at his wife, he storms off
to watch television until dinner. His wife then turns around
and immediately unloads on their son for leaving his shoes in
the middle of the floor. The boy gets mad and kicks the cat.

We Have Learned to Ignore It

Emotional abuse is like the parable—pervasive, self-perpetuating, and so common that everyone can relate to it. In fact, that's part of the problem: it is so common. Being a part of the cultural, social, and personal landscape, it has come to be ignored. As long as anyone can remember, Grandpa talked that way to Dad, who talked that way to Junior, who in turn talks that way to his own kids.

It probably seemed as if your family wasn't the only one that related this way. The neighbors down the road could often be heard yelling at their kids in the summer when the windows were left open. The kids on the street would escape their houses, meet somewhere, and swap horror stories about their parents.

Perhaps you grew up thinking that adults always dealt with kids that way. You learned to survive the yelling matches and to duck when the blows came. Or you just left to get out of the way. Whoever said life was fair anyway? Tragically, more often than not, even though you hate the way you were treated, you find yourself doing the same thing with your own kids, especially when you are stressed out or tired.

As you were growing up, the sarcastic remarks, negative messages, and disrespect shown you may have seemed part and parcel of your relationship with others in your family. It was just the way everyone spoke to each other. You thought you had learned to deal with it, to let it roll off your back and not bother you. All of the evidence you could see seemed to indicate that the way you were treated was normal. It might not have felt good, but that was normal too.

Even turning on the television bolstered this image that your life was normal. For those old enough to remember, the show *All in the Family* in its heyday gave weekly examples of verbal put-downs and sarcastic remarks, with the wisecracking, ill-tempered Archie constantly putting down his wife, his daughter and son-in-law, his co-workers, and his neighbors. Later came the foul-tempered Al Bundy in *Married with Children*. Even in this "enlightened" day and age, the use of verbal put-downs and sarcasm is still used to provoke laughter. In the cartoon show *The Simpsons*, the father is portrayed as a bad-tempered man constantly yelling at his sarcastic, wisecracking kid, who in turn takes great pride in his ability to outsmart authority figures and who constantly lives down to his father's poor expectations. Homer spends each episode reminding Bart frequently and loudly of just what he thinks of him.

Even if we consider ourselves enlightened, we sometimes find ourselves laughing at this abusive treatment. Why do we laugh? Because the abuse makes us tense up inside; laughter releases some of the tension. We can watch from the sidelines, in control, and experience the release and relief because we are not the victims. We can comment on the exaggerated foibles of Archie, Al, and Homer, and console ourselves that at least what we went through wasn't as bad.

Like a constant ringing in the ears or background noise, the frequency of emotional abuse has caused us to try to ignore it since we can't ever seem to get away from it. And if we can ignore it, we can deny not only its existence but also its effects.

We Have Learned to Deny It

Connie was forty-three years old and miserable. She didn't have any energy and was depressed all the time. Her life seemed to be one long black tunnel. She thought it was because her children had grown up and left home. She kept telling herself she just didn't have enough to do anymore to keep busy. She had married young and never held a "real" job; instead, she had stayed at home and raised her children. After the last child moved out, she had occupied herself at first by compulsively cleaning the house and using up her days in little projects. But lately even that was becoming pointless. The energy to keep up an empty house had dissipated along with her joy.

Some of Connie's friends urged her to go out and get a job or volunteer her time at a library, school, or hospital. But Connie was convinced she could never handle a "real" job since she had always stayed home. Her husband's reaction to that suggestion had been immediate—she had no skills, and who would want a fat, middle-aged woman for anything? Besides, lately she couldn't even do her housework or have a hot meal on the table when he got home. He was really afraid for her. If she did get a job, he knew she would be fired in no time at all.

At first Connie's husband's words had hurt her feelings, but deep down she knew he was right. He was just trying to save her from the embarrassment of failure. All the time growing up she had heard how she was stupid and slow, that all she would ever be good for was having babies. She knew then that her parents hadn't really meant to hurt her; they were just trying to save her from having unreal expectations about what she could do with her life.

And they had been right. She had never been good at anything except raising her kids. That was the only thing she had ever done right, the only thing she could take any pride in, and now her kids were gone.

Finally, Connie had sunk so low she sought help for her depression. If someone could only help her figure out what to do with the rest of her life, she would be happy and able to function again. But instead of looking at what to do with her future, Connie was guided by her therapist into looking at her past. For every example, past or present, that she could think of in which she had been emotionally abused, Connie was able to come up with a perfectly good reason to deny the negative and destructive nature of those messages, to excuse the abuse and, by extension, the abuser. After all, those who had been the most abusive to her had also been those she loved.

Since childhood, Connie had denied the truth about herself. She had denied the truth about her parents and how they treated her. She had even denied the truth that her children had always been more important to her than her husband. To her children she was somebody, but to her husband she was nobody. In order for Connie to truly get on with her life, she had to rethink her pattern of denial and recognize that what she had experienced as a child and as a wife was wrong, even if everything she had ever learned said otherwise.

Central to this ability to outwardly ignore emotional abuse is the denial of its true nature and negative impact. Often two negative, abusive messages that reinforce the emotional abuse are passed on to children:

1. Whoever is in authority over you (be it parent, spouse, or boss) can speak to you however he or she sees fit, no matter how negatively. Not only is it that authority figure's right to address you as he or she desires, but it is probably for your own good.

2. "Sticks and stones may break your bones, but words can never hurt you."

These messages are delivered not only by power-hungry individuals bent on subjugating all those around them but also by everyday people who learned those messages themselves and never thought to question conventional wisdom.

Historically, the view has been taken that those who are strong or who hold a position of power are justified because of that position or strength in whatever action they choose to take against a weaker or subordinate individual. Ancient conquerors took slaves of vanquished peoples as a matter of course. Feudal landowners dictated all aspects of the lives of their indentured peasants. Husbands could routinely beat their wives and children with impunity.

As civilization took hold and daily relationships came under scrutiny, oppressive behavior was identified and frowned upon. After World War II, the United States didn't enslave Germany or Japan; instead, they were rehabilitated. Employers today have government-regulated standards in business to protect workers. Men are now arrested for spousal abuse if they beat their wives and for child abuse if they beat their children.

While society has gone a long way toward making such outwardly aggressive behavior illegal, often it has turned a blind eye to the more subtle forms of oppression. While governmental and work relationships have been scrutinized, the family relationship has been considered private until recent years. A man's house was his castle, and a man's family was his to rule as he saw fit as long as he didn't physically or sexually injure his wife or children. Parents were given a wide berth to treat their children as they desired. They were, after all, *their* children. It has only been in recent memory that women have stopped being thought of as property and only within the last several decades that anyone has considered children as individuals separate from their parents.

As this new awareness has taken shape and behavior that was tolerated in times past has become criminal, it has been the violent, the sexual, the obvious behavior that has been targeted for reappraisal. The woman who gets drunk and beats her child is now put in jail. But the same woman who gets drunk and spends an hour yelling at her child for trivial or imagined misbehavior is exercising her parental authority.

In addition, many cultures in the world today still hold the view that the dominant person in a relationship has the right to control that relationship. The husband is in charge of his wife. The mother is in charge of her children. The employer is in charge of the employee. The cultural acceptance of dominance in relationships allows for emotional abuse to take root. In most of these relationships there is a necessary component of authority that requires responsibility. But authority over a person has been twisted into domination. To paraphrase an old axiom, "Absolute power corrupts absolutely and leads to abuse."

We Have Learned to Accept It

Only recently has our inner being, our emotional self, been recognized and given value. In a physically demanding world, emotions were for the weak, for women and small children. Emotions were something you were supposed to grow out of. Emotional women were thought to be out of control. Sto-icism was the preferred way to deal with the world. Straight-faced men and women were portrayed as strong, taking on the world and not letting it get to them. Little boys were taught not to cry or release their emotions as they got older. It was believed that part of the maturation process was learning to suppress one's emotions.

Children were told they needed to be tough to get on in this world. Physical wounds by necessity would hurt, but children were to steel themselves so that harsh words would simply bounce off their toughened hide. "Sticks and stones may break my bones, but words can never hurt me" was the child's standard boast if another person verbally attacked him or her. Since this way of dealing with each other was so common, there was nothing special about being subjected to it. What was special was how well you could get beyond it, how well you could deal with it and not let it affect you.

You were taught to take the verbal attack head on, slough it off, and go on with your life, throwing your indifference back into the faces of those who taunted you. Words weren't supposed to hurt you. If they did, there was something wrong with you. You had allowed someone else to gain the upper hand over you. You were weak, and therefore you deserved to be spoken to or treated in that way. In any case, if you were hurt, it was your fault.

Many of those I have worked with over the years learned to accept the world as it was given to them. They learned to accept relationships as they came to them. They looked around and saw the same thing happening to others, so they accepted what happened to them as simply part of life.

Since the abuse seemed so normal growing up, people will

often attempt to re-create that normalcy in future relationships. A man who has been verbally abused all of his life by his mother may, without thinking, be attracted to a woman who is loud and sarcastic. He doesn't see her behavior as strange or wrong. In fact, it will seem quite normal to him. He accepted the abuse as a child and continues to accept it from his wife as an adult.

We Have Learned to Perpetuate It

Bill and his wife, Margaret, brought to our counseling center their teenage son, Kevin, who was becoming increasingly rebellious and hard to control. He was throwing things around in his room, staying out late with friends whom Bill did not accept, and coming home drunk. After running out of options, and on the advice of their son's school, they sought professional help to sort out their differences.

Bill was convinced that a therapist would tell Kevin to clean up his act, learn to behave responsibly as a near-adult, and stop engaging in his destructive, disobedient behavior of staying out late and partying. Bill believed that a professional would help Kevin jettison his childish behavior and learn to accept the realities of the adult world.

Bill thought the therapist would deal only with Kevin's behavior. He'd pretty much had enough of trying to talk to his son. Their talks always seemed to end with them yelling at each other at the top of their lungs. Bill was determined to bring Kevin's behavior under control, and Kevin was just as determined not to be ruled by his father anymore. Bill was looking to the therapist to provide weight and a second opinion to his attempts to reason with Kevin. Bill had prepared himself for being told about all the problems Kevin had. Although they would be difficult to face, these problems were a fact of their life. They had to be faced squarely and dealt with in an adult and responsible way.

Instead, Bill was challenged by Kevin's therapist to take a hard look at the way he was treating his son and the messages he was transferring to him. Bill had to turn his view around from the adult he expected Kevin to be to the child Kevin actually was.

Bill discovered that Kevin really did want to please him but felt he never could hit the mark. Frustrated after years of trying unsuccessfully, Kevin not only had given up but in anger had rebelled against everything he knew his dad wanted him to be. Bill learned that the anger Kevin was feeling had been brought on by a deep sense of loss that he could never gain his father's approval.

Kevin discovered that Bill really did love him—so much so that he wanted him to be perfect so that nothing bad would ever happen to him, and so that if it did, he would be tough enough to handle it. Kevin learned that Bill was raising him just the way Bill himself had been raised.

Bill realized how powerful his words and messages were in Kevin's life and how much Kevin needed positive, affirmative messages from his dad in order to grow and function. Bill learned it was okay to show Kevin his love, his fears, his hopes, his emotions.

Kevin learned to begin to trust his dad.

As with other types of abuse, emotional abuse can be self-perpetuating. You accept the abuse, deny its impact, and ignore your inner self so much that, if you are not alert and careful, you end up continuing the cycle within your own relationships. Either you again take up the role of the abused in your new relationship or you switch roles and become the abuser.

Connie, the woman I wrote about earlier, perpetuated her abuse by initiating and continuing in a relationship with someone who reinforced the negative messages she had received as a child. Controlled as a child by her parents through the abuse, the thought of independence later in life was frightening and foreign.

Bill perpetuated his abuse by becoming the abuser, repeating the abusive patterns he had learned as a child on his own son, seeking to control his son and his son's response to the world.

Ultimately, any abuse is about control or the fear of losing control, and emotional abuse is no different. The abuser uses the abuse to take or keep control over another person.

- The husband who constantly tells his wife that she is stupid and can't do anything on her own is trying to keep his wife totally dependent on him, controlling the possibility that she might someday leave him.

- The mother who overshadows her daughter in all of her activities—picking out her friends, her clothes, her school—is trying to gain control over time by living through her daughter.

- The manager who stifles all creative thought at the plant, who issues endless instructions to his employees, who keeps a constant eye on all of the work in the office, is trying to control the possibility that someone beneath him might someday rise above him.

In each relationship, the abusers have learned techniques to control those underneath them and have no problem using those techniques to get what they need or think they need. People who have such a deep-seated need to control events and other people are operating out of a terrible sense of insecurity and are afraid of life and spontaneity. The unpredictable is something to be feared and controlled. Often the most unpredictable thing in their life is the people around them, so they must be controlled at all costs.

Emotional abuse, while often the product of a person who has an obsessive need for control, can also come from people who are simply out of control. For whatever reason, they have given up trying to have order in their life, to discipline their words and behavior. They use their words and actions to vent all of their frustrations and anger at the world they see around them and the past they can't get beyond. Life as they see it has given them a raw deal. They're mad, and everyone's going to know it. As the old saying goes, "Misery loves company." They're too tired or too defeated to keep their anger to themselves, so they vent it on whoever happens to get in their way. Tragically, the reason for the anger and the bitterness often comes from having been abused themselves.

Emotional abuse has been ignored, its effects have been denied, and its place within relationships has been accepted. The people doing the abuse may not even be aware of the harm they are inflicting on others. They assume that's the way it should be because that's the way they were brought up; there's nothing wrong with it. They assume that the control they are trying to exert over others is for their own good. Those who work with the inner being of the individual know and understand how destructive those assumptions have been in the lives of people.

It's time we stopped ignoring the emotional abuse that goes on around us. It's time we stopped denying that what we have experienced or practiced ourselves is really destructive behavior. It's time we stopped accepting abusive treatment of anyone, no matter who is doing it or to what degree it is taking place. It's time we stopped perpetuating the abuse that has been so destructive to ourselves and our relationships.

A Time to Heal

It's difficult to speak up for what's right. Usually we just stay silent and hope our silence will keep us under the radar of the person who is in the wrong. If we speak up, we will be noticed, and noticed people are targets.

Actually, all people are targets to an emotionally abusive person. It's a myth that you will be able to avoid abuse if you are compliant or perfect or quiet. The abuse doesn't stop; it can intensify. That is why it is so important to take a stand against abuse wherever it is found. The commonality of emotional abuse has been used as an excuse for silence far too long. To heal from emotional abuse, you need to begin to call attention to it, especially as it relates to your own life.

1. What is the first age you remember emotional abuse taking place? What was the pattern, and who was doing it?

2. How did you cope with the emotional abuse? Do you remember what you told yourself about it?

3. How did the abuser's words and actions make you feel about yourself?

4. Was this type of behavior pretty common in your extended family? Did you grow up in a household and family where "everyone" spoke and acted this way, from aunts and uncles to cousins and grandparents?

5. In your family, how were people in general treated—visitors to your home, salespeople and clerks in stores, servers at restaurants, callers on the phone? What did this teach you about the worth and value of other people?

6. As you look over the signs of emotional abuse in the last chapter, what behaviors have you come to accept as normal, as just the way life is?

7. Take a look at your present words and actions toward others. What are some areas of personal improvement?

8. In thinking about emotional abuse, how does ignoring it, denying it, or accepting it lead to perpetuating it in your own life?

9. As you think about the emotional abuse you've experienced in the past, what reasons have the abusers—or you—used to explain away hurtful behavior? Write down each reason.

10. For each reason above, ask yourself, *Is this a legitimate reason, or is this an excuse to explain away or minimize the hurtfulness?*

11. Is it easier for you to think that someone else has only an excuse, while you have a legitimate reason for the same behavior?

12. Have you ever considered that a family pattern of speech or behavior you've adopted is hurtful to other people?

13. If there are hurtful patterns you're perpetuating, are you ready to let go of them, apologize for them, and change?
14. If you find you're not ready to do that, what needs to happen for you to be ready?
15. Please sign and date the following statement of affirmation:

"I am committed to raising my self-esteem and not allowing others to abuse me. I will change my own patterns of behavior in order to break the cycle of emotional abuse."

_____

Signature

Emotional abuse is so common because we have allowed it to continue. Affirm today to do everything you can to make it an anomaly in your relationships, not a constant.

3

Why Is Emotional Abuse So Damaging?

Emotional abuse is so damaging because it outlives its own life span.

Robert is thirty-two years old and has trouble holding a job. He grates on people's nerves with his abrasive, blunt outbursts of displeasure at their behavior. Because of his inability to deal effectively with others, Robert is most successful at jobs in which he can work alone. Unfortunately, while Robert works best alone, he also works slowly. He constantly second-guesses his own judgments on the job. Caught up in daydreams, he spends a good portion of his time imagining how people will react to his work and what he will do and say in response. He wants to be ready for what he knows will come. Expecting and even anticipating a negative reaction, he seems to enjoy it, since it vindicates what he has believed they were thinking all along. He is happy inside because he was right. To others, Robert comes across as defensive and hostile because he is already sure that any response to him will be negative.

Robert grew up as the youngest of three children. His older siblings couldn't relate to his childish behavior. He was raised with the indelible impression that his brother and sister were smarter, better looking, and bound to be more successful than he could ever hope to be. His parents loved him, but Robert always had the sense that he was an afterthought, that the real tradition of the family would be carried on by the older, more capable children.

In school, Robert was always teased by the other children who knew his brother and sister. He was a thin, unattractive child whose dour expression set up a barrier without him speaking a word. Robert seemed to want to be left alone, and others were more than happy to oblige.

Robert grew up feeling that he would never amount to anything, that who he was as a person was not valued, and that people would always deal with him in a negative manner. Anticipating their reactions, Robert sought to beat them to the punch by being openly hostile and abrasive in all of his relationships.

Even therapy was a battle zone as far as Robert was concerned. He didn't like his therapist, didn't like her conclusions, and didn't like having to change the way he had always dealt with the world. Robert didn't want to take the chance of being hurt, yet neither did he want to continue living the way he was living now.

Robert's recovery will be slow, but as long as he listens to the truth, which softly whispers above the clamor of his self-doubt that he really is a valuable person, one day Robert will finally believe it.

Emotional abuse is so damaging because it outlives its own life span. Not only does it damage a person's self-esteem at the time it is done, it also sets up a life pattern that daily assaults the inner being. Present events and relationships are filtered through the negative messages and events of the past. Behavior is unknowingly modified to produce results consistent with the established life pattern. Through continued emotional assault, even a healthy life pattern can be subverted by an abusive one.

Damaging Effects of Emotional Abuse

When you view life as unstable, anxiety, tension, and fear result.

When you are constantly vigilant to the behavior of others, hypersensitivity and hostility result.

When you learn to second-guess yourself, confusion and feelings of disconnection result.

When nothing you do ever seems to be right, insecurity, guilt, and shame result.

When others tell you that you are always wrong, indecision and inaction result.

When you stop having the energy to fight it all, apathy and depression result.

When you have finally had it, rage results.

When you never seem to receive fairness, justice is all you think about.

When you have been hurt by those you love, love is viewed as a risk.

When living is painful, addictions are acceptable because they numb the pain.

When the mind is a jumble of emotional chaos, the body and its systems break down.

When your inner turmoil produces outer stress, your current relationships are endangered.

When you can't control your negative emotions, you become the very person you hate.

Don't ever let anyone tell you that emotional abuse isn't damaging.

Lack of Emotional Security

At the most basic level, emotional abuse robs you of your sense of security and value. In an attempt to bring order out of chaos, even the regularity of abuse can be substituted for a sense of what is normal.

One of the deepest needs of children is for consistency, including the certain knowledge that they are unconditionally accepted and valued by those who love them. Small children crave the repetitive, constant nature of certain stories in which the same words or phrases are used over and over again. Children learn what to expect, anticipate with delight the coming use of the word or phrase, and feel in control of the story when they can repeat along with the storyteller the right words at the right time. Toddlers will often ask for the same book to be read over and over again until parents are so sick of it they could just scream! What is boring to adult minds may be very comforting and affirming to children. The story always ends the same way. Life has order. By knowing the ending in advance, children have a sense of security and safety. They learn how it feels to be right, to know what lies ahead, and this produces a sense of control.

With emotional abuse, whether through purposeful or inadvertent neglect, children soon learn that anything is possible. They never know the ending in advance. There are no boundaries for behavior directed toward them or attitudes thrust upon them. And where there are no boundaries, there is no security. A study of children's reactions to physical boundaries on their school playground found that when a fence was present in their school yard, they happily played right up to its crisscrossed edges. They knew where the boundary of their world was and took advantage of every inch; it allowed them to relax and play in safety. When the fence was removed, the children huddled together close to the school building and did not venture down the hill to where the fence had been. Without the fence, they did not have a clear sense of boundary, of security. Instead of the removal of the fence promoting greater freedom, it produced heightened anxiety and unpredictable behavior. The presence of the boundary brought freedom. Removal of the boundary brought fear.

When a child lives in a household in which there are no boundaries on adult behavior, fear is the immediate result. Never safe, never secure, the child learns to expect and anticipate the sudden, the violent. A physical or verbal blow can come at any time. Accomplishments can be met with apathy, passive-aggressive indifference, or outright aggressive disapproval. It is best to be left unnoticed. Life is safer that way.

Fear/Anxiety

A loss of security leads to an ever-present feeling of anxiety or fear. When you are in the midst of being emotionally abused, you have a very real fear of how far the abuse will go and how damaging it will be. You cringe and hope against hope that it won't go on as long as last time or that at least it won't be any worse.

You learn there are no safe moments. Your abuser may be absent, but he or she may reappear at any time. What met with an apathetic response yesterday may meet with violent outrage tomorrow. You are robbed of the security of anticipation. Unlike the child who knows the right words that come at the right time in the story, the abused child knows no right words, and there never seems to be a right time. Besides, the storyteller never tells the ending the same way twice. No order, no sense can be made of the events swirling around you. You fear what each day will hold.

The human mind has a fascinating need to form order out of chaos. Visually you have an ability called *closure*. If you look at a picture that has some of the lines and details missing, your mind fills in the blanks so completely that you actually think you have seen the whole picture. You haven't; you have just seen parts, but you have been visually fooled into thinking you saw what wasn't actually there.

In the same way, your emotional makeup strives to produce closure on the bits and pieces of what happens to you. When you don't know why things happen, you fill in the blanks. The oppressive anxiety and fear you feel must have a reason. What is happening to you must have a cause. Too often your abuser is ready to supply you with one—not the right one, but you don't have the capacity to know that. A reason is provided for the abuse, and you accept it.

Guilt/Shame

The reason given for the abuse varies: you are bad, stupid, ugly, or unwanted, or you are the wrong sex, the wrong age, or the wrong whatever. No matter what reason is provided, *you* are to blame for what is happening to you. You are guilty of causing the abuse.

The guilt you are feeling is not true guilt. True guilt is brought on by a realistic understanding of your behavior and its consequences to yourself and others. False guilt is an oppressive burden that is not based on reality but on the warped views, ideas, and attitudes of others. Emotional abuse transfers those warped views onto you, and those warped views produce mind-numbing, action-paralyzing shame.

For some people, assuming the guilt for the abuse might seem to be a devastating decision—and it is—but it also has some very practical uses. For the person who has been emotionally abused, guilt is born out of a sense of fear of the world and what it holds. At first it makes no sense that this should be happening, but then guilt takes over. You feel responsible. You are told you are responsible. Some of the nameless chaos is encapsulated. *Bad things happen to me because I am bad.* A sense of order is established. By latching onto your guilt, you are really attempting to take back control of your life.

If I am guilty of causing the bad things that are happening to me, then all I have to do is change my behavior, my looks, my weight, to stop causing the bad things. To children this is a very logical conclusion. It is a way of asserting that they really do have some control over the way they are being treated.

At first, children who are abused in this way will attempt to control their behavior so completely that they do nothing that angers their abuser. They will often appear to be model children—compliant, quiescent, extremely adult acting. They are praised by other adults for their behavior. They begin to hope that they have found the key that will stop the abuse.

Hand in hand with false guilt is false hope—hope that if they are just good enough, thin enough, bright enough, or hardworking enough, the abuse will stop and the people who are supposed to love them will finally start acting in a loving way. By accepting the mantle of guilt, the child expects a payoff in hope. *If I can be the way you want me to be, then you will love me.* If the person who abuses them will change and love them, the crushing weight of guilt and shame can be lifted.

Just as your eyes deceive you with closure, your heart can deceive you with false guilt. You can so completely see the proof of your own guilt that it affects the very mental image of yourself that you carry around inside. You are guilty. You are bad. You deserve the awful things that happen to you and that people say to you. You are right to be ashamed of the way you are. Something is wrong with the world if you are not punished. The overwhelming feeling of guilt becomes what is normal. If others do not punish you, you will punish yourself so that order may be maintained. You will desire to create what you were used to enduring and used to feeling. In essence, better the hell you know than the heaven you do not.

Tragically, the abused child accepts guilt and endures shame to buy hope, hope that he or she can control the situation. The human heart has a tremendous capacity to hope.

This is especially true of the heart of a child, because there is still plenty of room for hope to stretch its edges. The scarring of disappointment hasn't started to restrict and bind.

As year after year of disappointment builds, as time after time the abuse has continued no matter what the abused child has done to control his or her behavior, the abused heart will begin to harden. Hope can no longer find a suitable home. Disappointment leads to frustration and anger, which result in resentment slowly creeping in.

> *I'll never be good enough.*
> *Mom will never like the way I look.*
> *I'm too fat for anyone to ever love me.*
> *I'll never be smart enough to get a real job.*
> *I guess Dad was right when he said I'd end up on the streets.*

Hope hasn't worked. It was false all along. Controlling your own behavior hasn't worked. The abuse continues. Disappointment and resentment must now be contended with. But they rarely come alone.

Anger

When security is gone, when fear must be dealt with on a daily basis, when the oppressive weight of guilt and shame crushes the spirit, when hope is extinguished in the rush of despair, often the only way to respond is with anger. The injustice of the abuse eventually demands the response of rage from the battered psyche of the abused person.

This rage and anger can be explosive and consuming,

taking opposite directions upon release. Often in the abused person this anger is directed inward. Presented daily with "proof" of total unworthiness, the emotionally abused can turn the frustration on themselves. In my practice I have seen children who habitually injure themselves. They will hit their heads repetitively on a wall with almost hypnotic ferocity. Their frustration and anger, having no other outlet, is released on their own bodies. The physical pain they feel becomes a way of purging their all-consuming anger and emotional pain.

For bulimics, the very act of purging either by vomiting or laxatives is a violent physical expulsion of these negative emotions of guilt, shame, frustration, and rage. I have also worked with people who release their anger by secretly cutting themselves on their arms and legs. The pain and release of blood become a metaphor of their need to rid themselves of the toxic buildup produced by emotional abuse.

Depression

It is said that depression is only anger turned inward. Emotionally abused people often give up on emotions, since emotions have proven to be so damaging. They have been beaten down by the emotions of others and struck through the heart by their own emotions in response. No safety, just anger, fear, shame, and guilt. *Perhaps*, they think, *if I punish myself there will be no need to be punished by others.* Or, *I'm only getting what I really deserve.*

It takes a great deal of energy to deal with emotional abuse and stay buoyant. Each emotional assault takes its toll on that store of energy. Some people simply run out of strength to climb the mound of abuse heaped upon them. When that happens, they slip into the pit of depression. Unable to escape from anger, fear, shame, and guilt, they attempt to shut down all of their emotions. With no visible way out, they curl into themselves, isolating themselves from others and imploding their world.

Rage

This resulting anger can take another route to expression in the emotionally abused. When they finally have had enough, they can vent their own anger and aggression on the person who has abused them. In today's society there is a legal condition being used as a defense in murder and injury trials known as the "battered woman syndrome." It depicts a woman who has been so emotionally, physically, and/or sexually abused by a lover or spouse that the only way she can see to remove herself from the situation is to actually kill her abuser. In a violent, uncontrollable act of rage, she attempts to reestablish control over her life by killing the man who has been controlling her through his abuse.

This dramatic act is not the norm, however, for those who have been abused. More often I have found the anger directed inward, or if the anger is directed outward, it usually is not directed at the person who caused the abuse. Often that person is absent from the abused adult's life, either by distance or by death. Usually the abused has continued the life pattern by maintaining relationships with an abuser of some kind. The anger is then transferred to a different relationship—a spouse, a parent, a child, or even a co-worker. Wherever it is transferred, the results are the same—a desperate attempt to control or influence others in improper ways, such as passive-aggressive manipulation or a domineering attitude.

However it is manifested, a tremendous feeling of rage is characteristic of those who are abused. For the most part, it is kept tightly locked away, out of sight. To let it escape would mean to face the rancid reality of failed hope, so it stays tightly controlled year after year, bound and hidden, while the rest of the personality makes the transition from child to adult.

A lack of security brings about fear, which brings about guilt and shame, which perpetuate false hope, the death of which produces anger and depression. Fear, guilt, and anger—these are three of our most powerful emotions. Emotional abuse is so damaging because of the way it sets a person up to deal with these three powerful emotions.

Fear, guilt, and anger are not negative emotions. Emotions, in and of themselves, are not good or bad, positive or negative. They are simply reactions to the world around us. The positive and negative (or good and bad) labels result from how we have learned to deal with our natural emotions. Fear prompts a child not to put her hand on a hot burner. Instead of being negative, fear has kept her from serious injury. Guilt over hitting another child prompts genuine remorse and a desire to control emotions in the future. True guilt, instead of being negative, is helping to mold future appropriate behavior. Anger at seeing an injustice take place has often motivated someone to change the course of history by his or her response. Far from being negative, anger has provided the fuel to keep going in the face of adversity.

In order to mature into healthy, well-adjusted adults, all children must learn how to deal effectively with the fear, guilt, and anger they feel. These are powerful emotions that can be used for much learning and good when harnessed properly. It is hard enough in normal households to learn how to react to these emotions wisely. All of us, if we are honest, could probably admit that we are still learning how to deal with our own fear, guilt, and anger.

Someone who has been emotionally abused is left to feel all of these emotions—not only those that have been produced appropriately but also those that have been produced inappropriately by the abuse they have suffered—without the adult guidance and help to put them into perspective.

- How can a child go to an adult for help with an unnatural fear when the very thought of how that adult might react produces an even greater fear?
- How can a child reach out for forgiveness and perspective in dealing with guilt when all she has been told up to this point is how worthless she is?
- How can a child receive love and forgiveness for reacting in rage and anger when the response of choice from the adult is a verbal tongue-lashing?

Not only are emotionally abused children left to come to grips with these emotions themselves, they are also overloaded with anger, fear, and guilt through the actions of the adults around them. Not only do they not see the proper response to these emotions modeled by those around them, but they also see the improper response put forward as the example they are to follow.

People who were emotionally abused as children have a real problem dealing with fear, guilt, and anger as adults. Their childhood has been damaged by the abuse they have suffered, and their adult lives have been sabotaged as well. Emotional abuse is particularly damaging because of this continuing effect. I have seen very specific ways the damage of emotional abuse is manifested in adults. They often are directionless in life; they develop adult abusive relationships; they have unexplained physical symptoms; and they experience spiritual isolation.

Adrift

When persons have undergone significant emotional abuse in the past, they have learned that actions have negative consequences. As adults, then, they can have difficulty making decisions and taking action. Often these are highly capable people who have developed the misconception that they are doomed to fail or that success is attained only through perfection. Since perfection is virtually impossible in their eyes (or more accurately through the eyes of their abuser), failure is assured. It is only in the "planning stage" that success is a possibility. Therefore, either they will remain stuck in the "planning stage," endlessly planning for the future with no action, or they will choose ill-thought-out actions and jump from thing to thing, hoping to find success.

Tom came to work with me at The Center for Counseling and Health Resources at the behest of his wife. She couldn't understand why Tom wouldn't stay put in one job. She had a good-paying job as a teacher, but as the children grew and their financial needs increased, she needed Tom to "settle down" and produce a more reliable income. She was frustrated at his continued attempts to jump from one job to another, from one "financial opportunity" to another. He always had great plans for how this next thing was going to solve all of their financial challenges. The problem was, as soon as he would start it, off he would go on another tangent and never complete what he started. This was becoming a real problem in their marriage, and she wanted Tom to address it.

Tom came to The Center after starting and stopping counseling with three other people. But his wife had threatened divorce, and Tom realized he was running out of options. In therapy, Tom came to realize how damaging past emotional abuse had been. Growing up, Tom could never seem to get the approval of his father. He tried endlessly to find something he was really good at in order to force his father to give him the attention and validation he so desperately needed. He tried sports, music, school clubs, and other extracurricular activities. And he tried to find a subject in school that came easily.

Trying something new became second nature for Tom. But once he started an activity, the fear that he wouldn't be able to measure up with this new thing grew and grew. Soon it escalated to a panic stage and Tom could no longer tolerate continuing in the activity. Terrified, he would run away to the next planning stage, the next activity. He carried this pattern of behavior into adulthood, producing a sporadic, uneven, hectic employment record that made finding a decent job even more difficult.

Over time, we worked with Tom to understand the seeds of this behavior and work toward redefining success in a job. We helped Tom learn to relax and not panic. He came to trust himself more and listen to the whispers of his childhood emotional abuse less and less. His employment situation didn't fix itself overnight. Tom started at a job he had always considered "beneath" him and through it learned consistency and dependability. Then he began to advance within the corporate structure.

Radar Love

It seems that some people have an uncanny ability to attract the "wrong" kinds of people in relationships. I have heard clients describe themselves as having a "radar" whereby the wrong kind of people seemed to be able to pick them out in a crowd. *Why*, they want to know, *do I always seem to attract someone who is going to hurt me?* The answer to that question too often lies in a pattern of emotional abuse. Someone who has been emotionally battered as a child often chooses to enter into abusive relationships as an adult. These can be platonic or work relationships, but most often they are "love" relationships. Some are looking to try to "rewrite" the past by forcing an abusive person to change and actually love them. This compensates for the pain of a past relationship in which change never occurred. Some are subconsciously seeking an abusive relationship in the present to mirror an abusive relationship in the past. Some are so beaten down by the emotional abuse in their past that they are convinced that an abusive relationship in the future is the most they can ever hope for—at least it's a relationship. Some look for a relationship in which they can assume the role of the abuser as a way to vent their rage at being victimized in the past. Whatever the reason, one of the most common consequences of emotional abuse in the past is an unhealthy relationship in the present.

In a way, some people do emit a sort of relational radar by broadcasting in subtle ways their willingness to enter into an abusive relationship. Those who are abusers and are looking to abuse in a relationship know how to ensnare someone who has been damaged by emotional abuse. The abuser will initially lavish attention and affection on the person, carefully avoiding the presentation of his or her true, cruel nature. Only after snagging the person with the bait of care and concern will the abuser begin to show the depth of his or her true abusive nature. If the person responds by remaining in the relationship, the hook is set and it becomes difficult and painful to leave. It takes great courage to admit that you have made a mistake in love and to end an abusive relationship when you have been emotionally compromised by abuse in the past.

Heart Sick

Study after study shows that stress is a destroyer of health, causing disease and disability. The emotional toll of abuse is manifested in physical stress. Anger, guilt, and fear produce specific physiological reactions that wear down the body. Over time this stress produces physical symptoms that are impossible to ignore or medicate. These can include:

digestive difficulties including ulcers and irritable bowel syndrome

heartbeat irregularities

chronic fatigue

tightness of the chest

difficulty breathing or hyperventilation

muscle tension or shakiness

headaches

loss of appetite

binge eating

chronic illness such as colds or flu

yeast infections

panic attacks

jaw disorders such as night-grinding of teeth and temporomandibular joint (TMJ) syndrome

high blood pressure

A visit to your primary care physician or dentist is certainly warranted in these cases, but the emotional causes may not be addressed or discovered. When Julie came to The Center, she was experiencing depression over the way her body was breaking down. Julie thought it was age and excess weight. While these were contributing factors, the most startling complication I could see was her total lack of joy. Every physical pain was examined, experienced, agonized over, cataloged, and charted. These Julie could deal with. What she had a harder time accepting was how she was substituting a focus on the physical for the emotional—which was threatening to break down after years of verbal and mental abuse, first by a mother who couldn't be bothered by an unplanned child and then by a husband who couldn't be bothered by the trophy wife for his business career.

With Julie, we began a whole-person approach that addressed the physical symptoms she was experiencing along with addressing her deep-seated emotional anguish and pattern of abuse. Julie rediscovered health and joy, and each supported and enhanced the other. Her depression lifted, her physical symptoms improved, and Julie learned to love herself again.

Soul Sick

In the whole-person approach we utilize for healing at The Center, we incorporate the spiritual side of each person. Often those who have undergone a pattern of emotional abuse have withdrawn from any spiritual connections. This is especially true if the emotional abuse took place in a home that was also "religious." Unfortunately, religious faith has been used as an abusive weapon in relationships, from parent to child and from spouse to spouse. In such homes, God is presented in the context of an all-powerful, punitive, vindictive being, taking on a supersized persona of the abusive personality. When authority in the family is used to subjugate, the ultimate authority—God—may be negatively viewed. This negative view continues on into adulthood, leaving the abused person fearful of or hostile toward God. Distance is desired, barriers are erected, and spiritual isolation occurs.

This is all the more devastating because God, the source of true love and enduring comfort, is not considered a viable avenue for healing and restoration. Guilt and shame may still dictate that the person go through his or her pattern of religious ritual, but the life-sustaining connection to God is never consummated. As part of our whole-person recovery, we encourage clients to discover afresh who God is, separate from the misconceptions created in their abusive situations.

God ceases to be a larger version of an abusive parent and becomes their heavenly Father, the one who loves them eagerly and unconditionally. Such clients come to understand their true identity as the bride of Christ—beloved, cared for, and died for.

A Time to Heal

As you can see, the effects of emotional abuse can be wide-ranging and often subtle. In order to help you identify some of these effects in your own life, I'd like you to think about and answer the following questions. Please realize you may be able to answer yes or no quite strongly for some, but for others, you may need to think about whether the statement is true, is not true, or has some element of truth to it. Really think about your answers, and make sure to highlight any that produce an especially strong reaction.

1. When you think about your future, do you feel a sense of anxiety and uncertainty?
2. Have you learned to expect the worst from life?
3. When good things happen to you, are they met with suspicion, as if they'll turn out not to be true or real after all?
4. When good things happen to you, do you feel unworthy?
5. Are you willing to take risks in life (for example, in your career, your relationships, or your activities)?
6. Is it difficult for you to accept thanks or praise?
7. Are you constantly aware of and alert to the emotions of others?

8. Are you constantly aware of and alert to the opinions of others?

9. Do other people's opinions matter more to you than your own?

10. When something goes wrong, do you assume others will blame you?

11. When something goes wrong, do you assume responsibility, even if it wasn't your fault?

12. Do you find it difficult to make decisions?

13. When you do make a decision, will you change it if opposed by someone else?

14. Do you find yourself avoiding situations in which you'll need to make a decision?

15. When in a group of people, do you avoid the role of decision maker?

16. Do you find yourself working primarily for the approval of others?

17. Do you consistently neglect your own needs in order to fulfill others' needs?

18. Are you more comfortable fulfilling others' needs than addressing your own?

19. Do you find yourself getting angry at the way other people take advantage of you?

20. Do you feel that your family and those close to you take advantage of you?

21. Do you get angry at yourself for your shortcomings?

22. Are there times when you just want to get away from people and all their expectations of you?

23. Do you fantasize about telling people off?

24. Are there days when life just doesn't seem worth it?

25. Do the demands of life sometimes seem too overwhelming?

26. Do you find yourself erupting in anger at small, insignificant things?

27. Do you find yourself erupting in anger at people you come into casual contact with, such as store clerks, phone solicitors, bank tellers, or other drivers?

28. Do you feel your anger is justified?

29. Is it hard for you to get and keep a job?

30. Do you choose jobs that are "safe," where too much won't be expected of you?

31. Are you working in a job you dislike?

32. If you dislike your job, are you afraid to leave?

33. If you leave your current job, do you assume no one else will want to hire you?

34. Are you afraid you can't live up to others' expectations?

35. Do you view a promotion at work with fear—as a risk that could lead to failure and demotion?

36. Do you feel taken advantage of by your employer?

37. Do you feel undervalued or unappreciated by your employer?

38. Do you dream of winning the lottery or hitting the jackpot as a way out of your present circumstances?

39. Do you find yourself turning to outside things (for example, alcohol, drugs, cigarettes, gambling, television, video games, food) as a way to make you feel better inside?

40. Do you consider these activities necessary to help you cope with life?

41. Do you consider these activities a reward for past or present struggles?

42. Are you fearful of entering into relationships with other people?

43. Are you convinced you will end up giving more to the relationship than the other person?

44. Are you suspicious of why the other person would want to be in a relationship with you?

45. Are you grateful for anyone who would enter into a relationship with you, even if his or her behavior isn't the best toward you?

46. What behaviors are you willing to tolerate to be in a relationship with another person?

47. What behaviors are you unwilling to tolerate to be in a relationship with another person?

48. Do you enter into a relationship based on how being with that person will make you feel about yourself?

49. Do you feel validated as a person by being in a relationship with someone else?

50. Are you afraid other people would find you unlovable if they really knew you?

51. Do you feel you need to hide your true self in order to maintain a relationship?

52. Do you feel tired and run-down most of the time?

53. Do you feel like your body and health are a hindrance to your life?

54. Are you angry with your body for how you look and feel?

55. Do you feel helpless to change your body or health?

56. Do you suffer from anxiety or panic attacks?

57. Do you live with a fear that something terrible could be wrong with you?

58. Do you avoid going to the doctor for fear of what might be discovered?

59. Do you see your doctor on a regular basis for relief from a series of vague, chronic health conditions that are difficult to pinpoint?

60. Do you feel God has abandoned you?

61. Do you feel God has abandoned you for good reason?

62. Do you blame yourself for God's abandonment?

63. Have you been taught that God loves you?

64. Do you believe that God loves everyone, just not you?

65. Do you feel distant and removed from God?

66. Are you fearful of God's notice and scrutiny?

67. Do you believe in God's grace and forgiveness?

68. Do you think you need to be a better person than you are now before you can come close to God?

Think about the questions you've just answered, and look over the effects of emotional abuse listed in this chapter. Complete the following statements regarding the effect emotional abuse has had on your life.

1. The effects I feel most strongly at the present time are
   _____.

2. The effects I remember feeling as a child are _____
   _____.

3. When I think back on the abuse I have suffered, the emotion that most comes to mind is _____
   _____.

4. When I think about the abuse in my life now, the emotion that most comes to mind is _____
_____.

5. When coping with these emotions, I frequently use
_____.

6. The one consequence I most want to work on and recover from is _____
_____.

7. In order to do this, I confirm that I will undertake the following three actions to make my life better:

    a. _____

    b. _____

    c. _____

Now, don't stop there. Take a look at all the effects of emotional abuse you've identified. Go through and number them by the present, direct impact they have on your life. Your goal, as you continue to read through this book, is to put together a support system—whether family, friends, pastors, or health-care professionals—to begin to help you address these issues.

Affirmation Statement: "My victory comes by building my self-esteem higher than the effects of emotional abuse. I confirm that each day I will rise above the abuse and choose actions that show I am able to love myself."

Part 2

Types of Emotional Abuse

4

Emotional Abuse through Words

The power to demand obedience is a great responsibility. When we obey others, we submit to their will above our own. Therefore, this power should be used sparingly and only with the other person's best interests in mind.

Words can be powerful tools or powerful weapons. The weapon of choice for emotional abusers is often verbal. They use their words to control, to wound, to entrap, to humiliate. Through their words and tone of voice, they imprint messages on the minds of those who hear. These messages, repeated often and forcefully, infiltrate to the inner being of their victims, shaping the way they view themselves.

While each person is different, there are several distinct methods the emotional abuser can use to dispense his or her abuse. It may be a single form or a combination of forms; however, most are recognizable. As you read through this chapter, think back over people you have known. You probably will be able to come up with at least one name for every pattern of verbal abuse.

The Overbearing Opinion

Carrie hated going shopping with her mother. If she wanted to go to Old Navy, her mother insisted they travel to Sears. If she chose a pink sweater to try on, her mother would loudly proclaim that blue was a *much* better color on her, and besides, a blouse was much more practical than a sweater.

If Carrie started dating Josh, her mother would manage to mention three or four times how much more suitable Mark was. She had a thousand reasons why Josh just didn't quite come up to her high standards.

Before Carrie left for school, she prayed her mother would be preoccupied and wouldn't notice what she was wearing, how much makeup she had on, what time she was leaving, or who she was planning to meet after school. Carrie's mother had an opinion about *everything*. It never seemed to correspond with what Carrie was thinking.

All of her life, Carrie moved within the shadow of her mother's opinions. Nothing was ever insignificant enough for her mother to be neutral about. From the temperature of the room to the volume of the television to the position of the chair, Carrie's mother altered her surroundings to fit her preferences. Other people simply were not consulted.

As a child, Carrie soon learned that it did no good to argue or attempt to explain her own opinions to her mother. Carrie felt her mother just wasn't interested in what she thought. Depending on her mother's mood, confronting her could bring disastrous consequences. It simply wasn't worth the risk, not for Carrie or for anyone else in the family for that matter.

Resigned to always keep her opinion to herself, Carrie discovered as an adult that she had a hard time making decisions.

Distrusting her own opinions, she would often look to someone else, a dominant personality, to validate her own thoughts and decisions. As a child, Carrie had learned she wasn't a competent judge.

I once saw a sign that read, "Everyone is entitled to their own opinion, as long as it agrees with mine!" This is the essence of the overbearing opinion. The sign I saw was in jest, but for the emotional abuser, this is a life statement. It defines how he or she views the world and everyone else in it.

Healthy discussion, on the other hand, allows for the expression of a variety of opinions on any given subject. Few things can be said to be black or white in reality. Most opinions are very personal and are derived through experiences, knowledge, and personal preferences. Because individuals are unique, the opinions they arrive at will necessarily be different. This brings variety, contrast, and flexibility, all of which enhance healthy relationships.

We communicate through facts, opinions, and feelings. Facts are just that—indisputable segments of reality. "The sun is out, the sky is blue, and the birds are singing" could be facts about a day in the park. We also communicate through opinions. "It certainly is crowded here today" and "This is the best park in the city for taking a walk" are opinions based on experiences, knowledge, and personal preference. Finally, we communicate our feelings. "It makes me happy to see the ducks swim in the pond" and "I love to walk in the grass without my shoes on" are statements of feelings.

Statements of fact, the first example, rarely come under dispute. But opinions and feelings, the second and third examples, are subjective observations. They are personal perspectives on the day in the park.

The abuser with the overbearing opinion restricts the flow of free expression, treating his or her opinions and feelings as if they were as incontrovertible as facts. The personality of the abuser is superimposed onto the abused, stifling the abused's ability to bloom on his or her own. This robs the abused of the experience of trial and error, of exploring his or her own thoughts, likes, and dislikes.

Healthy give-and-take in relationships allows for an honest, gentle exchange of feelings and opinions. But when opinions or feelings are forced on us, we resist and often rebel. Not only are we not allowed to have our own thoughts, but we are forced to accept unfamiliar or unshared ones.

The Person Who Is Always Right

Mike cringed inside. He stood waiting for the words he had heard so often in his life. "I told you so," his father said with a tight lip. His dad was furious, and Mike set his jaw, clenching his teeth. It would only be worse if he blurted out what he so wanted to say: "Yeah, you're always right! You're never wrong about anything!" Once, just once, Mike wished he could prove his father wrong.

Mike's father had told him the car wasn't in good shape when he had bought it, but Mike really didn't care at the time. He just wanted the car. Halfway into his dad's lecture about why the car was a stupid idea, Mike had tuned him out. Somewhere between the explanation of the fuel system problems and the bald tires, Mike had stopped listening and started hoping—hoping this time his dad would be wrong.

Now Mike had to admit it: his father had been right about the fuel pump, though he really hadn't listened to what Mike was trying to tell him. Mike knew the car wasn't perfect, but it was a good deal anyway. It might not have been the car his father would have chosen, but Mike was still happy with his choice, fuel system problems and all. No matter what Mike tried to say, his dad wouldn't listen. His dad was right about the car, and that was all there was to it.

Hand in glove with the overbearing opinion is the person who is always right. Overbearing-opinion abusers have an idea or opinion about everything. People who are always right do not make the same volume of pronouncements, but when they do, they always position themselves in the right and everyone else in the wrong. They will sift through events and information for proof of their rightness, bombarding anyone who questions them with a list of reasons why they are correct in their thinking. There is no room for a second opinion.

Neutral in circumstances in which they have no interest, these abusers are tenacious whenever they feel compelled to render a decision. *What* is right is not the important thing so much as the *fact* of their rightness. Even when normal people would admit an error, abusers who are always right will find a way to justify their decision. If it cannot be justified by the circumstance, they will often manufacture a plausible reason. In other words, even if the event turned out wrong, they were still right.

Unlike the overbearing-opinion abuser, the person who is always right allows other people to have differing opinions. If the other person is shown to be right, that is often met with a studied indifference—as if it wasn't that big a deal in the first place. However, if the other person is wrong, the failure is pointed out strongly and loudly.

Living with a person who is always right produces frustration and anger. Events are constantly being turned around in his or her favor. You begin to think there is no justice in the world, since your abuser never has to admit his or her error. More important, you may also begin to believe that your abuser has been right all along. Like living with an overbearing-opinion abuser, you begin to second-guess your ability to make decisions, for they never seem to be the right ones. Or you make decisions that are obviously the wrong ones because you figure you are going to be wrong no matter what you do. In order to declare your own independence, you will intentionally choose an action you know is wrong.

Realistically, no one is always right or always wrong. All of us are plenty of both. In healthy relationships, forgiveness is extended when someone is wrong and graciousness is shown when someone is right.

The Judge and Jury

When Darlene was sixteen years old, she entered therapy through a court-ordered decision. After she was caught shoplifting at a local department store, the judge had decided to see if family counseling might alter Darlene's classic path toward juvenile delinquency. She hadn't wanted to come, but Darlene was quite used to absolute decisions and pronouncements.

Darlene's father was the unwavering decision maker in the family. It didn't matter what anyone else decided; everything was dependent on whatever ruling her father laid down. The whole family could have planned something as simple as a night out for dinner, but if Father decided he was too tired, they all stayed home. If Mother had said it was all right for Darlene to spend the night at a friend's house but Father didn't want her to be gone, she just couldn't go. No arguments, no amount of persuading could change his mind once it was set. His decisions were final. No appeals process. Verdict reached and decision rendered. Period.

Darlene soon learned that her father's decisions usually had very little to do with the circumstances and very much to do with how he was feeling at the time. If he was in a good mood, he could be generous. If he was in a bad mood, all bets were off. There was no reliable standard, only convenience or inconvenience, for her father's decisions seemed to be based most often on what the situation meant to him. If he had to drive her anywhere, forget it. If it meant he had to leave the house after he got home, forget it.

Darlene learned to filter all her decisions through her father's what's-in-it-for-me lens. She learned not to consult anyone else about what she had decided to do. If he didn't know about it, he couldn't stop it. Darlene learned to hide her activities from her parents. Consequently, some of Darlene's choices were inappropriate ones, and she wound up in court.

All of us can probably think of a person who acts as if he or she is the sole judge and jury for making decisions. Akin to the person who is always right, the judge-and-jury abusers allow no opposition to their will. The judge-and-jury abusers not only make the decisions, they also make the laws. What might be a reason for doing something on Monday may cease to be a reason on Tuesday. A decision doesn't necessarily need to be "right" as long as it fills their needs in other ways. They are not as concerned with the process of the decision as they are with the outcome of the decision—which is to have happen what they want done.

The right or wrong of what judge-and-jury abusers decide is irrelevant. To them the most important thing is their position, to be in control of the people around them. It is their call to make, whether good or bad. Others are to obey them, not because they have rendered a good decision, but because they are the authority.

In healthy parent-child relationships, children have to learn to obey their parents' decisions, often without total understanding of why those decisions are made. Small children learn that adults are authority figures who need to be obeyed. A toddler shouldn't stop to question an adult decision that he get out of the street. Such obedience can be very important for the safety of the child, especially if a car is traveling in his direction. However, the judge-and-jury abusers use the obedience of others not for good or safety but for their own comfort or control.

The power to demand obedience is a great responsibility. When we obey others, we submit to their will above our own. Therefore, this power should be used sparingly and only with the other person's best interests in mind. Power should never be misused for personal comfort, gain, or control.

The Put-Down Artist

"So, you really think you can get that job, huh? What a joke! Why in the world would anyone want to hire you?" Jeff's older brother sneered at him with disgust.

"Well, I guess because I'm a hard worker and I'm willing to learn," Jeff responded angrily, feeling that familiar knot tying up in his stomach.

"Hard worker? Right. If you're such a hard worker, how come you don't get better grades?"

Jeff felt like he had been hit in the stomach this time. "My grades aren't that bad. I do the best I can!"

"I'll let you in on a little secret, kid," Dennis got up right next to him, put his arm around his shoulder, and whispered loudly, "Your best isn't all that great!"

"Maybe not," Jeff replied, twisting out of his brother's arm, "but I'm trying for that job anyway!"

"Perfect!" Dennis exclaimed, throwing himself back down on the couch and turning up the sound on the stereo. "Now all my friends can go see my little brother wearing a dweeb hat, bagging fries. 'May I take your order, sir?' What a joke! . . . Hey, kid!" he yelled as Jeff left the room muttering under his breath. "Try not to fall into the fryers!"

Emotional abuse can come from different sources in a variety of ways. Some of the most destructive abusers are people who habitually put down another person through their words. Instead of using their speech to encourage and lift up the other person, they use it to crush and discourage. Their use of language and their tone of voice are purposely chosen to degrade the feelings of the other person, to make them feel valueless. It is almost as if their words become a verbal heel grinding down the self-esteem of the abused.

There is nothing veiled or subtle about this form of abuse. It connects with the intensity of a right hook to the jaw. There is never any doubt how these abusers really feel about their victims. Their speech is littered with verbal garbage spewed directly at the abused. It does no good to duck. It will always find its mark.

Put-down artists attempt to bring themselves up by pushing everyone else down. Usually their degree of self-contempt is evident in the intensity with which they degrade others. Whatever the reason for the abuse, its effects are still the same for the abused. Life becomes a verbal minefield where anything you say can and will be used against you at any time and for any reason.

If you are a victim of a put-down artist, you learn to suspect all relationships. A casual word, a thoughtless remark by anyone else, is immediately taken as a personal insult, a maddening slight on your sense of self. The result for the abused is suspicion and hostility in dealing with other people. There are no comfortable, relaxed relationships and no humor. Everything is taken literally and negatively. This form of emotional abuse is the verbal equivalent of a physical beating and a form likely to accompany actual physical abuse.

All of us have spoken something in anger that was meant to hurt someone else. But in healthy relationships, those instances should be rare. Even when those angry words come, there is a deposit of good words and healthy interaction to draw on so the rash remark can be put into proper perspective, apologized for, and forgiven.

The Stand-Up Comic

"Jane's such an airhead, it's a wonder she doesn't float away completely!"

"Did you hear what Bob over in engineering did the other day? He was so busy figuring up his gas mileage, he ran out of gas!"

"Like Shirley really deserved that raise! Like she's so hard-working! The only thing she ever worked hard for around here is making the most of her coffee breaks!"

"What a moron Joe down in the garage is! The only way he's gonna move up in the world is to climb on top of a car!"

The stand-up comic is just that—only the butt of his jokes is always you. You are his perpetual straight man. He doesn't laugh *with* you, he laughs *at* you. Through sarcasm and exaggeration, he beats down your self-image.

Very similar to the put-down artist, the stand-up comic uses twisted humor. It's not enough to insult you; the insult must be witty. Where the put-down artist makes use of a club, the stand-up comic uses a whoopee cushion. The jokes are often in public where his or her humor encourages others to participate in your abuse. After all, it's just a joke, and the stand-up comic is very clever at finding what is considered funny in any given situation.

Everyone seems to be laughing, so how come you don't think it's funny? Because the humor is being gained at your expense. The humiliation you feel is the fuel for the sarcasm and jokes. Your shame energizes your abuser.

This kind of abuse provides the abuser a way out, an instant excuse for any injury caused. After all, if you are the only one who isn't laughing, there must be something wrong with you. Everyone else seems to be able to take a joke, so why can't you? Furthermore, this type of abuse can leave a deep sense of outrage at being used for another person's pleasure.

The abuser gets all the laughs, and you are left to feel humiliated. Often the only defense against this type of abuse is to become a clown yourself, beating your abuser to the punch by beating up on yourself. Better to be the class clown than the verbal punching bag.

While it is important to a healthy self-image to be able to laugh at yourself and your foibles, it is not healthy to allow yourself to be used as the punch line for other people's jokes. There is nothing funny about the way that kind of abuse makes you feel.

The Great Guilt-Giver

I first met Renee when she came reluctantly into my clinic. She couldn't have weighed more than eighty pounds. Her face was skeletal, skin drawn back over protruding cheekbones on a body made pencil thin by forced starvation. Even in her condition, Renee was convinced she was hideously fat.

It didn't take long for me to uncover why Renee was trying to destroy herself. Renee was living under the burden of tremendous guilt. After all, if it hadn't been for her mother becoming pregnant with Renee, her mother might have gone on to become one of the premier dancers in a prestigious dance company on the East Coast. If Renee's mother hadn't put on fifty pounds while pregnant with Renee, she might have been able to get back into shape after giving birth. If Renee's father hadn't left soon after Renee was born, leaving Renee's mother to go to work full-time, her mother might have had the time and energy to practice and find another dance company to work with. If it hadn't been for Renee, life might have been so much better for her mother.

So there was Renee: eighty pounds and trying desperately to be thin enough to fit the mold of a dancer. Eighty pounds and trying desperately to make up for all the damage she had done to her mother's life. Eighty pounds and dying from the load of guilt dumped on her by an unhappy, unfulfilled mother.

While the jokes of the stand-up comic can hit you all of a sudden like a ton of bricks, the weight of the guilt-giver comes on a brick at a time, just long enough for you to adjust to the weight before another one is added. Brick upon brick of guilt, year after year, message after message, remark after remark. Usually not delivered in haste or loudly, but with a sigh, with a sad, disappointed look that communicates that you are the cause of all of his or her problems. If it weren't for you, life would be so much better.

If you were emotionally abused in this way, you may feel as if you have no importance to your abuser. In fact, you may feel as if the abuser's life would be so much better if you weren't around to mess it up. Nothing could be further from the truth.

For guilt-givers, the most important person in the world is the one on whom they heap their guilt. Without you, they would be responsible for their own failures. For whatever reason, life hasn't turned out like they wanted it to. But instead of being realistic about their goals and their own part in fulfilling them, they have chosen to shift responsibility from themselves onto you. The load of their own guilt is so crushing to them that they habitually shift some of it onto you. Faced with accepting responsibility themselves or harming you, they choose the latter.

Without you, there would be no one to draw recompense from. With you feeling guilty and at fault, there is always a way for you to "make it up" to the person you have "harmed." Maybe it's by never leaving them to form other relationships. Maybe it's always being there to do that errand, pay that bill, or take care of whatever problem arises. After all, it really is your fault that they find themselves in such a mess in the first place. The least you can do is fix it for them.

Healthy guilt causes us to evaluate our actions and respond accordingly. Every one of us is guilty of some wrong behavior within a relationship. We're human—we make mistakes. True guilt is the response. It causes us to feel sorry for what we have done, accept responsibility for the damage, and do what we can to repair it.

Guilt-givers do not use true guilt. By manipulating the facts, they produce false guilt. The guilt is false because it is based on false information. Renee was experiencing false guilt because her guilt was based on the "fact" that her birth ruined her mother's dancing career and thus her entire life. The truth both Renee and her mother needed to come to understand was that Renee's mother had made a choice to get married and leave her dancing career for her husband. When he left her, she was unable to return to the devoted life of a dancer because she was caring for an infant. The real truth was that the decision to stop dancing was her mother's, not Renee's. Renee had no say in the matter.

False guilt is slippery. Because it has no basis in truth, the reasons behind it can be altered by the abuser. If one reason stops working, another one can be substituted—whatever it takes to produce the desired guilt reaction. True guilt, on the other hand, can be met head-on, dealt with, worked through, and forgiven.

The Preacher

Carl knew it was coming. The real question was how long it would last. Depending on what kind of day his dad was having, it could be a few minutes or a half hour. If he didn't have to bring back his progress report signed by a parent, he wouldn't even have showed him his grades. Carl might have asked his mother to sign, but he knew her response would be, "Show your father." Might as well get it over with.

Carl shifted from foot to foot as he stood by the kitchen table watching his father read over his grades and teachers' comments. His father was silent for quite a while as he read over the report. That wasn't a good sign. *Great*, thought Carl, *just what I need*.

Fifteen minutes later the "sermon" was over and Carl was released. His legs and back ached from having to stand still and listen to all the reasons he had disappointed his father, his family, his teachers, even God.

Preachers have a sermon for everything you do. Preachers are used to controlling and manipulating people by their words. Often they love to hear themselves talk. They don't so much communicate with other people as preach at them. They can be compelling and charismatic, and often they invoke religious themes in their speeches. They use these "sermons" as a way to pontificate on the faults of the person specifically and the world in general. Any small infraction, to preachers, has earth-shattering implications. Their words and messages are grandiose and meant to make the listener feel contrite and moldable. Invoking the name of God in their speeches reinforces the "rightness" of their point of view. It also makes it impossible to argue with them, for arguing with them equals arguing with God.

The Historian

Judy was ready for a fight. She had come prepared. All her ammunition was stacked up and ready to be fired. The powder was primed and just looking for a spark to set it off. She had had a bad day at work. She had gained three pounds over the past week without eating *anything* wrong. Besides, she had the perfect excuse—her period was only a few days away. Tense and angry, she felt ripe to explode.

A couple of days earlier, Judy's husband had made an off-hand remark about a dress she was wearing looking a little tight. Granted, she had asked him what he thought of it. Ever since, she had been stewing about his answer.

When he walked in the door from working outside, she hit him full blast. "Get those muddy shoes off my clean carpet this minute!" Jumping back as if stung, her husband looked down at his footprints, barely visible on the rug.

"Aw, come on, Judy; it's not so bad. Here, I'll take them off for you."

"You never care about the house! All the work I do around here you just take for granted!"

"No, I don't," he began to protest. "Besides, how many times do you compliment me on the yard work?"

"I did two times last week. Once on Thursday morning on the way out to the car, and the other time was Sunday when you brought in the bouquet of flowers." Judy lobbed two shells in his vicinity. "When's the last time you said anything nice about the house, huh?"

"I always tell you how nice the house is!" her husband replied, confused.

"Oh yeah? When was the last time?"

"I don't remember every single time I say something nice to you." Taking off the shoes was forgotten as her husband tried desperately to search for a bunker behind the kitchen counter.

Judy followed, relentless in her anger, sensing she was gaining the historical upper hand. "Well, I remember every mean thing you've said or done to me over the past ten years!" Shells arched across the kitchen tiles.

"You remember everything!" her husband fired back. "It doesn't matter how insignificant, or how much I said I was sorry, or how much you provoked me. I don't even remember saying or doing half of what you say I did!"

"Are you saying I'm lying?" Judy demanded, full of righteous indignation. Direct hit.

"No!" her husband protested, angry and confused.

It seemed to turn out like this every time they fought. He would get so turned around he couldn't even remember why the argument had started in the first place. All he could remember was the sickening feeling of dealing with Judy in one of her rages. He felt lost and out of his element. She would bring up stuff he had said years back. He couldn't remember why he had said it or if he had even said it at all. Judy never seemed able to let go of the past. And her version of the past was always so much worse than he remembered.

Historians are a *This Is Your Life* nightmare. They are people who, like Judy, remember every bad thing you have ever done or they think you have done. With computer accuracy, all your bad moments are logged and recorded to be brought up in full detail at any future time the historian deems appropriate. There is no getting beyond an event, no putting the past behind you and going forward. Like a heap of heavy luggage, historians drag all of it along with them.

Historians' view of the past is decidedly one-sided. They never seem to remember their own faults or mistakes with the same clarity they recall yours. If you bring up one event in your defense, they can come up with a multitude of others to bury it in a verbal barrage.

This type of emotional abuse is dangerous because historians seem to be presenting facts. They back up those facts with details: dates, places, and actual conversations. It is easy to become overwhelmed with the information and give in to the demands of this type of abuser. But often the "facts" being presented are actually the abuser's opinion of what you said and why. A word, a phrase, an intonation can be changed to produce a completely different intent than the one you had when you said it. It isn't so much *history* as it is *historical fiction*, based on the truth but altered for dramatic content.

In healthy relationships, the positive and happy memories are those that survive. The others are dealt with and forgiven, and the relationship is allowed to continue on. Each of us makes mistakes on a daily basis. If these mistakes were merely piled up on top of each other, they would soon bury us. Historians can't forgive and forget, nor do they want to. Their manipulation of the past helps them to control people in their present and future.

The Silent Treatment Abuser

Sylvia entered the quiet house. When she had pulled up in the driveway after work, she hadn't seen any lights on in the front of the house, but Jim's car was parked in its normal place. So he *was* home. It meant he was in the den at the back of the house instead of in the living room. *What have I done now?* she thought to herself.

Jim always retreated to the den when he was mad at her. The more she bothered him and tried to find out what was wrong, the longer he would stay inside, not speaking to her. It was best if she just went about her business in the house as quietly as possible, trying to stay out of his way and waiting for him to either snap out of it or blow up and tell her what she had done wrong. She couldn't force him to respond, and over the years she had gotten used to his behavior.

No discussion of emotional abuse through words would be complete without including the absence of words as a form of abuse. This is commonly known as "the silent treatment." Abusers punish their victims by refusing to speak to them or even acknowledge their presence. Through silence, the abusers loudly communicate their displeasure, anger, frustration, or disappointment. Depending on the person, this silent treatment can last for hours, days, or weeks. For some abusers, it is a preferred method of communication because of its ability to humiliate and control the victim. It is used most effectively by those in close relationship, such as a spouse, parent, or child. The silence, the loss of verbal relationship, is meant to exact an emotional toll on the other person, who often will go to great lengths to attempt to restore communication with the abuser. This level of control is precisely what the abuser is looking for, as well as a way to vent his or her anger at the other person. By not verbally expressing that anger, by "avoiding" showing anger, the abuser is allowed to feel as if the victim is the only person at fault for whatever wrong is perceived by the abuser. If the victim responds to the silent treatment with anger, the abuser is doubly vindicated.

Turn Up the Tape

Verbal abuse is like a tape recorder that never stops playing. On and on the messages run, over and over, year after year. You hear the words in your head whether you want to or not. They repeat themselves softly in the quiet moments when no one else is speaking. Like relentless waves undermining the sand, they steadily wash away the foundations of self-esteem and self-respect. Too often they become the background noise of our lives—too quiet to be clearly heard, too loud to be totally ignored.

As unpleasant as it may seem, the only way to deal with verbal abuse is to turn up the recorder. Really listen to what those messages are saying to you, find out when they were recorded and by whom, and begin to erase them by taping over them with positive, uplifting, encouraging messages of self-esteem and self-worth that come through healthy relationships.

A Time to Heal

Conventional wisdom may teach that "Sticks and stones may break my bones, but words can never hurt me," but we know better. We know that words have the power to hurt or help, wound or heal. God, who spoke the first word, reveals this clearly through Scripture, where words are compared to everything from sharp swords to smooth oil, from being harsh to being sweet as honey. As we think about the power words have had in our own lives, let's first take a look at God's truth about the power of words.

Psalm 55:21 speaks of how people can say one thing with their mouths but mean something completely different in their hearts: "His speech was smoother than butter, but his heart was war; his words were softer than oil, yet they were drawn swords" (NASB). This is so true when pronouncements of comfort and love are in word only and are followed by deeds that testify to anything but.

In Psalm 57:4 King David articulates the plight of those who are trapped under the influence of verbal abuse when he says, "I am in the midst of lions; I lie among ravenous beasts—men whose teeth are spears and arrows, whose tongues are sharp swords." This is especially haunting to me, as I have heard these thoughts and fears expressed by verbally abused children. These children and adult children truly feel devoured in spirit by the verbal abuse suffered—sadly, too often by those given to them by God with the charge to love and protect them.

Psalm 64:2–3 reveals the power of words and the true nature behind the motivation to harm with words: "Hide me from the conspiracy of the wicked, from that noisy crowd of evildoers. They sharpen their tongues like swords and aim their words like deadly arrows." In the hands of the wicked, words become the weapons they use to launch harm against another.

Proverbs 15:1 says, "A gentle answer turns away wrath, but a harsh word stirs up anger." Verbal emotional abuse is the harsh use of words that produces anger. It is this built-up, unresolved anger that festers inside a person, damaging self-esteem and poisoning relationships.

Proverbs 16:24 says, "Pleasant words are a honeycomb, sweet to the soul and healing to the bones." When honest affection and love are expressed through words, they bathe the soul in comfort. This comfort is desperately needed in this world and in all our relationships—and it is what emotional abuse utterly destroys.

A little earlier, in verse 21, this same proverb tells us that "pleasant words promote instruction." Too often, what passes for instruction out of the mouths of the verbally abusive is anything but. Whatever "wisdom" might be contained within their tirade is blasted apart by their abusive presentation. This brings to mind a grocery store scenario between a child and parent. True, it might be the fifteenth time the child has asked for something inappropriate from the grocery store aisle, but when the parent erupts in yelling and belittles the child for asking, what is being taught?

Here again are the behavior types outlined in this chapter:

- The overbearing opinion—whose intensity of opinion overshadows everyone else
- The person who is always right—who turns the words "I told you so" into a verbal indictment
- The judge and jury—who reserves the right to pronounce judgment on all actions on any given day in any given mood

- The put-down artist—who uses words to crush the spirits of others
- The stand-up comic—who laughs at you, not with you, and encourages others to do the same
- The great guilt-giver—who burdens others with false guilt for all of his or her own problems
- The preacher—who has a long-winded sermon, full of fire and brimstone, for every occasion
- The historian—who has a photographic memory for the lapses of others but a blind eye to his or her own shortcomings
- The silent treatment abuser—who transmits volumes of negative thoughts without saying a word

The words and phrases we use are very important, as is the way they are delivered. Yet often we are the most careless with this vital form of communication. Now that you have read over this chapter and identified verbally abusive patterns in others, take some time to consider the type of communication you have with other people in your life.

1. As you think over your life, how have words been used as weapons against you?
2. Have you experienced a time when the words of another were "softer than oil" but ended up wounding you deeply, as with a sword?
3. In reading over the different types of verbal abusers, did one or more stand out to you? If so, why?
4. Were you able to identify yourself in any of these examples?

5. Are there patterns of speech you have identified in this chapter that you'd like to change?
6. List the main types of verbal abusers you have dealt with.
7. What effect did their words have on you?
8. How do you feel about them today?
9. What lies have you believed because of their abuse? Be specific.

It's time to begin to reclaim the truth and put the lies to rest. As you think about the lies you have believed, think about the truth. What is the truth about you? Write down three positive, affirming truths about yourself.

1. _____
2. _____
3. _____

Most of the time, words roll off our tongues without our thinking much about them. It's time to consider our words carefully—what we say and how we say it. Perhaps the Golden Rule has no greater application than in the realm of communication. Internalize this statement: "I will strive to speak to other people the way I wish to be spoken to—with kindness, respect, and consideration."

5

Emotional Abuse through Actions

For some abusers, words are not enough. They choose to manipulate and control through actions as well. These actions can be their own actions, or they can be those actions imposed upon the abused.

Emotional abuse can come not only through words but also through the actions that accompany those words, such as physical intimidation, manipulation, and physical threats. Emotional abusers who use actions as well as words increase their arsenal of ways to manipulate and control. They attempt to control not only behavior but circumstances as well.

Tragically, emotional abuse through actions can result in domestic violence or physical abuse. But this is not always the case, and severe emotional abuse can occur without the abuser ever laying a hand on the abused. The abuser may lash out at objects or smash possessions out of rage. The abuser may withhold needed items or resources dispassionately out of cold calculation. In every incident of physical or sexual abuse, emotional abuse is present. Emotional abuse, however, can be present without overt physical harm. Yet danger lies in the escalating nature of emotional abuse. If someone is accustomed to abusing you emotionally, physical abuse is never far away.

The Commander in Chief

Dennis's father ran a tight ship. With military precision he controlled the lives of each member of the family. All had their assigned duties and responsibilities and were expected to carry them out with proficiency and efficiency. Slackers were not tolerated by Dennis's father, so Dennis made it a point never to be a slacker.

Life was a regimented routine at his household from the time the children were awakened for school to the minute the lights were turned out at night. Only occasionally were exceptions made.

Dennis's father liked order, and having other people participate in family decisions was messy. Dennis's mother went along with the program and backed up her husband in any dispute. The kids followed orders when they could and tried to cover up when they couldn't. Sometimes it worked; sometimes it didn't. Punishments were handed out with precision as well—a certain number of whacks for each offense when they were younger and a designated length of time for a privilege to be withdrawn when they were older.

Life was lived out as expected, and surprises were rare. There was consistency and order, but laughter and spontaneity were rare. There was physical discipline, but physical affection was rare. There was a sense of being part of a unit, but the sense of being a family was rare. Dennis couldn't wait to get out of the house.

Often emotional abusers will attempt to conceal the true purpose of their abuse—to control those around them. Commanders in chief, on the other hand, are completely open about *what* they are doing, if not *why*. They feel so comfortable in the role of controller, so confident in their ability to make the correct decisions for the people around them, so assured of their right of authority, that they openly direct the lives of others.

Unlike the judge-and-jury abusers, whose reasons for making decisions often fluctuate according to circumstances or comfort, commanders in chief maintain a rigid code of behavior not only for others but also for themselves. Life is not something to be enjoyed but something to be controlled. A relationship with this type of person is very difficult because it usually flows one way. Commanders in chief control the amount and type of interaction with others. While they may show their anger, they rarely show their uncertainty. Their image as controller must be preserved at all times. The old *Mary Poppins* song says, "A spoonful of sugar helps the medicine go down." It is so much easier to respond to authority when love and compassion accompany it. With the commander in chief, all you get is the bitter medicine.

Deprived of the affection and love you crave, you may rebel totally and live a life out of control, seeking comfort wherever you can find it. Or you may buy into the control and begin to pattern your own life as rigidly as you have been taught—rejecting any need in your life for physical affection or closeness, not allowing other people in to disturb the sterile order of your life.

The healthy use of authority in any situation provides structure and order. It should also allow for the free flow of ideas and opinions from all concerned with a coordinated source of decision making. When ideas and opinions are suppressed, emotional avenues are stopped up. Healthy authority creates structure. Unhealthy authority creates anger and frustration.

The Ventaholic

Jimmy's mom couldn't figure it out. All of a sudden her second grader didn't want to go to school anymore. Oh, he didn't just walk in the door and announce he was tired of school. Instead, he started making up excuses why he just couldn't go. First his tummy hurt, then his head hurt, then his throat hurt, then he was too tired. Bright in class, Jimmy had always liked going to school, not only for what he could learn, but also to see his friends and play.

Finally, his mom had had enough. Determined to get to the bottom of Jimmy's unusual behavior, she began to question him about school. "Why don't you want to go to school?" she asked him.

Jimmy rolled his eyes, trying to avoid hers.

"Are any of the other kids giving you a bad time?"

"No, they're fine. . . . I just don't want to go . . . that's all." He was clearly uncomfortable talking to her.

"But you have to go to school, Jimmy. Besides, you're doing great! Mrs. Reed says you're one of her best students." At the name of his teacher, Jimmy became tense.

"I just don't want to," he pleaded.

"Is there something wrong with Mrs. Reed?" his mother asked, sensing her son's discomfort when she said the teacher's name.

"No," he said quickly. "She's my teacher."

"I know she's your teacher, but do you like her, Jimmy?"

"Well, she's a good teacher, but there is something I don't like about her," Jimmy admitted.

"What don't you like about Mrs. Reed?" His mother felt like she was pulling teeth, trying to be patient and give him the time he needed to tell her what was wrong, though warning signals were going off in her head.

"She screams all the time." There, he had said it.

"I don't understand. What do you mean 'she screams all the time'?" Jimmy's mother had been in class a few times and had noticed his teacher had a tendency to raise her voice, but she assumed it was because she was nervous having a parent in the room. "I know when I've been in your class she's been a little loud, but there was a lot of talking going on."

"Mom," Jimmy said matter-of-factly, "it's ten times worse when you're not there. She yells at everyone, even if you're not doing anything wrong. If she even thinks you're doing something you shouldn't, she yells at you."

"I'm so sorry," she responded, taking her son in her arms. "Tomorrow I'll go to school and see the principal. What she's doing isn't right."

"Why does she yell so much, Mom?"

Most of us have had the unpleasant experience of being in the grocery store when a mother verbally unloads on a child. Usually she isn't even aware you are there, or else she doesn't care. Immediately you feel a rush of anger toward the parent and aching compassion for the child. Helpless, you watch and listen as the screamer vents her frustration on the cringing victim. But after the embarrassment is over, you can turn down the canned vegetables aisle and leave the unpleasantness behind you.

As hard as it is to hear such abuse, it is even more devastating to live with. The ventaholic is like a volcano that erupts in violent fits whenever the pressures of life get to be too much. As unpredictable as a real volcano, the ventaholic robs those around her of any sense of peace. It is the volatility of this type of abuser that produces an overwhelming fear of imminent disaster. Never safe, never secure—always on guard.

Anger or excitement causes our adrenaline to flow and increases the volume of our voice. The rush during a sporting event causes us to yell enthusiastically at the top of our lungs. We let out a scream of panic when danger presents itself. We snarl in anger when we are hurt or frightened.

For the ventaholic, adrenaline flows all the time. The actions of others are constantly interpreted as threats, and the reaction is verbal rage. This flush of emotion can be very addictive. When rage is vented, the person feels powerful, invincible, in control. Bottled-up feelings are unleashed, releasing internal pressure. The release can be physically pleasurable, creating a desire to repeat it again and again.

As we discussed earlier, anger is an emotion we all have. Depending on how we express it, anger can have positive or negative consequences. For ventaholics, anger is the emotion of choice. They are so filled with rage that it seems to spill out whenever they open their mouths. But anger of this kind is seldom spent. It seems to have an inexhaustible core. In fact, the more rage is vented, the more it is produced. Instead of venting to let off steam, the ventaholic uses anger to keep the pot always boiling.

This type of abuse is most tragic when it occurs between parent and child. If you grew up in a household where anger was constantly vented, in essence you were emotionally attacked. Every time your abuser opened his or her mouth, you knew what was coming. Your stomach knotted up and your teeth clenched, preparing to withstand the onslaught. There was no use talking back or speaking up in your defense. That only made the attack worse, adding fuel to the fire. It was better to shut up and take it, better to stuff your own anger than add it to the mix.

Anger is expressed even in healthy relationships, but anger should never be an end in itself. Instead, it should be a sign that something is wrong, that we have been hurt in some way, that something is left unresolved that needs to be dealt with so all concerned can go on.[1]

The Intimidator

"If you don't play with me, I'll take my ball and go home."

"If you say one word to Mom or Dad, I'll tell them you were in on it."

"If you don't go to bed this instant, there'll be no television for a week!"

"If you don't play dolls with me, I'll tell Mom you hit me."

"If you don't go along with these figures for the audit, I'll make sure you don't have a job tomorrow."

"If you don't do what I want, I'll leave."

"If you . . . then I"—the classic words of intimidators. Their control over your behavior is always issued in the form of a threat. Sometimes it is delivered at the top of their lungs. Other times it is slipped into a conversation on the wings of a whisper. However it is given, the threat is understood.

Intimidators can be of two types: the ones who are all talk with no real consequences behind their words or the ones who mean every word they say and back it up with action. Either way, they present an unhealthy means of gaining whatever it is they desire.

Consequences are a fact of life. If I do A, then B happens. On one hand, if I eat too many of the wrong foods, my body gets sick. If I stay up too late at night, I'm tired in the morning. If I don't do my job correctly, I could be fired. On the other hand, if I smile at someone, she may smile back. If I wake up in the morning deciding it's going to be a good day, it probably will be. If I do a good job at work, I'll most likely be appreciated. We all understand the role consequences play in our lives. The intimidator knows only the negative ones.

Each of us has a responsibility to those around us to explain what we need from them, how we feel about their actions, and what those actions mean to our lives. That's healthy. What is unhealthy is when those explanations become threats or battle lines drawn in the sand: "If you step over this line, then I'll deck you!" Boundaries need to be set in any relationship, and they should define the areas in which freedom can take place. Intimidators, however, are trying not to set boundaries but to erect barriers, to keep you from doing anything they don't like.

Threats are most effective when they are actually carried out. If they are, the threatened person learns to deeply fear the intimidator. If they are not, the threatened person loses all respect for the intimidator, and the intimidator often feels compelled to up the ante, leading to escalating threats of harm or violence. In healthy relationships, threats are not necessary. Trust and love provide the motivation for behavior.

The Roller Coaster

"Whose turn is it?" the oldest one asked. It was always her job to ask.

"It's not mine!" the youngest said quickly, shaking her head, eyes wide.

"It must be me," the middle child acknowledged reluctantly. "As soon as I know, I'll come back up and tell you."

"Okay," the oldest said, patting him on the shoulder. "Just make it seem normal."

"I know. I know." With that, he started down the stairs toward the kitchen. Mom was up, and it was his job to find out what sort of mood she was in. If she was in a good mood, he would know it pretty quickly, and he would run back upstairs to his sisters and let them know they could relax for a while. If she was in a bad mood, it might take a little longer to show up, but sooner or later he would catch it for something. Then, as soon as he could, he would go upstairs and prepare the others for the rest of the day. A good mood meant they could relax. A bad mood meant do everything you're told, don't argue, and, above all, don't get in her way!

These siblings rotated the duty every weekend. During the week they would rush off to school, so even if Mom was in a bad mood, they wouldn't be at home for long. And if she was in a good mood, there was no telling if it would last until they got home. On the weekend, it was especially important to know what kind of mood she was in. If she was in a good mood, maybe they could have a friend over, go to a movie, or spend the night at a friend's house. If she was in a bad mood, there would be chores upon chores to accomplish, all to her rigid standards, with little time for anything else.

Good moods were short but sweet, like a cool breeze on a summer's day. Bad moods were longer and had to be weathered like storms. The first child down the stairs was the lookout to see which way the wind was blowing.

The types of abuse talked about so far have been ones of consistency—the consistent rule of the commander in chief, the constant yelling of the ventaholic, the incessant threats of the intimidator. Roller coasters are just the opposite. They have huge mood swings. The only thing constant about them is their inconsistency. Just like a real roller-coaster ride, the upswings in mood can be exhilarating and the downturns can be terrifying. Yet this kind of abuse is scarier than a roller-coaster ride, because it is a roller-coaster ride in the dark. You have no clue which way the ride is going next. You just hang on for dear life and shift whenever you can.

The up-and-down mood swings of the roller coaster rob those around him or her of any sense of peace. The house is not a haven; booby traps are everywhere. Safety and security can be found only outside the home. School is safe. Friends are safe. But the roller coaster is not.

No one maintains an emotional plateau. We all have ups and downs as a part of everyday life. But a healthy self-image helps to regulate those mood swings and level out our emotional states. If we're up, we enjoy it and spread our happiness to others. If we're down, we get through it and try not to spread our unhappiness to others.

The Dr. Jekyll and Mr. Hyde

Donna lived a life of secrets. She existed in two worlds: one that encompassed her public sphere and one that encompassed her private sphere. On the outside, she appeared competent and pleasant, not overly friendly but hardly rude in any way. People basically commented that she kept her distance. Publicly Donna looked like she had her life together. Privately, Donna felt as if she were falling apart.

Growing up, Donna had learned to separate herself into two people. The one on the outside had it all together; the one on the inside didn't but only came out when she was alone. The outside person was collected. The inside person was a mess. Donna came to see me when she could no longer live two lives. Increasingly, the private person was coming out in public situations. Frustrated at not being able to maintain her composure any longer, she finally decided to try to put her halves back together.

As Donna shared her life with me, it became evident that she had learned this pattern early in life. Growing up with a strict Christian background, she had gone to church every Sunday she wasn't sick. Her father was a leader at church, and her mother was involved in a lot of church activities. Because of that, Donna and her siblings were expected to be always on their best behavior at church and around church people.

"Sunday best" meant more than just clothing as Donna was growing up. It meant changing how you acted. When

Donna was with her father at church, he would put his arm around her shoulders and brag about how well she was doing in school. At home, though, he would rant and rave about her failure to have A's in every subject. At church her mother spoke quietly and calmly to her, taking time in front of others to explain whatever it was she needed Donna to do. At home her mother was short-tempered and exasperated when Donna didn't immediately understand what was expected of her.

Donna had grown up in a "Dr. Jekyll and Mr. Hyde" home. And just like Dr. Jekyll, she learned to conceal the identity of Mr. Hyde at all costs. No one must know she lived with a monster.

Concealment, deception, gentleness in public but harshness in private—these are the signs of living with a Jekyll and Hyde. It could be your parent, your spouse, or even yourself.

All of us fragment ourselves to some degree. We are the child, the parent, the spouse, the friend, the employer, the employee, the teacher, the lover, the loner. We can have different moods depending on where we are. We can adjust our personalities to function under whatever circumstances we find ourselves. That flexibility is healthy. It is like our bodies responding to different levels of stress. Our breathing, heart rate, and blood pressure all react and change according to what is happening to us.

What is damaging is the denial of one aspect of our personality when we are functioning under another. When we're calm, we cannot deny we get angry. When we're happy, we cannot deny we get sad. When we're patient, we cannot deny we get impatient. When we deny certain aspects of our personality, we experience fragmentation. When fragmentation of the personality is taken to the extreme, it leads to the compartmentalizing of all of life's activities. In other words, when I'm in public I can only act and feel this way, but when I'm in private I can do whatever I want. When I'm in public I'll only show a certain side of myself to others, but when I'm in private anything goes. When I'm in public I'll wear a mask of serenity, but when I'm in private I'll rip it off to show the chaos underneath. When I'm in public I'll show that I love you, but in private I'll prove it's a lie.

Living with a Jekyll and Hyde means living with mixed messages. He loves me; he loves me not; he loves me; he loves me not—except it's not flower petals he's tearing off, it's pieces of your heart. Living with a Jekyll and Hyde means living a life of secrets. No one must know what your private life is really like.

We all come as a package deal. Parts of ourselves we like and other parts we don't. A prayer by Reinhold Niebuhr goes something like this: "God, grant me the serenity to accept the things I cannot change, the courage to change the things I can, and the wisdom to know the difference." By doing this, we grant ourselves and others unconditional love. We send the message, "You don't have to be perfect for me to love you, and I don't have to be perfect to love myself." We need to be less of a Dr. Jekyll and Mr. Hyde and more of a "what you see is what you get."

The Illusionist

"Bill is such a great guy!"

Carly smiled and made some sort of neutral comment. It did absolutely no good to dispute the evidence of Bill's obvious charm. He was engaging, witty, energetic, and charismatic. People liked him. She knew the feeling. When Carly first met Bill, she was overwhelmed by his outgoing nature. His gestures were larger than life, outlandish even. But to a young woman being courted, he seemed the walking incarnation of romance. She was being wooed. What she didn't realize was that while she was being wooed by Bill, she and everyone else were being fooled. Bill's grand gestures and protestations of care and love were for general audiences only. In the intimacy of the private viewing area called home, Bill turned out to be someone quite different.

At first Carly just put up with Bill's moodiness, nastiness, and withdrawing into himself. She figured he would snap out of it. It didn't take her long to learn that Bill's negative private behavior could turn in an instant if someone came over to the apartment. Finally, she mentioned to Bill her concern over the way he treated her at home as opposed to the way he treated her in front of others.

Bill's reaction was astonishment. He acted as if he had no idea what she was talking about. Every incident she brought up was countered with a rush of excuses, reasons, and outright denials as Bill fought to maintain the illusion of himself as the compassionate lover, the life of the party, the perfect soul mate. It struck Carly that Bill needed her only as long as she continued to mirror the reflection of himself he so needed to see.

Illusionists are generally highly intelligent, charismatic people who thrive on being seen well by others. As long as there is an audience, they are "on." Because it takes a great deal of energy to be "on," their "off" persona may be the exact opposite. In public they are witty and humorous; in private they are sarcastic and cutting. In public they are deferential and attentive; in private they are hostile and distant. In public they are happy and easygoing; in private they are sullen and angry.

Being in a relationship with an illusionist can cause you to doubt your own judgment. Because illusionists are generally highly intelligent, they are able to convince you, even in the face of contrary evidence, that the concerns you have are invalid. If there is a problem, you are always portrayed as the source. Feigning confusion, they appear shocked that you find their behavior unusual. If you ask other people, people who have seen only the carefully constructed illusion, you may not get validation of your concerns. Instead, you may hear a reiteration of how wonderful the illusionist is. Highly persuasive, the illusionist is very adept at creating and maintaining a positive image.

What is most important to illusionists is the maintenance of the illusion of who they are. You are valuable to them only when you are helping them to maintain this illusion. You become a danger to them if you question the illusion they have created. Because the illusion is more important to them than you are, the truth is never acknowledged. Your reality of events and circumstances is consistently denied, down-played, explained away, rejected. This is a pernicious form of emotional abuse in that it causes the abused to second-guess his or her own assessment of the relationship and the circumstances surrounding the relationship. As such, many will stay in the relationship for an extended period of time until their ability to help their abuser maintain the illusion demands too great an emotional toll. At this point, the abused person will leave but with his or her sense of self seriously tattered. After all, how could anyone leave such a great person? Because others have not seen through this illusion, the abused person who leaves can appear to be in the wrong. Not only does the abused lose the relationship, but he or she may lose any friends made during the relationship.

The Person Who Plays Favorites

Julie looked up and scanned the bleachers. Nope, he wasn't there yet. Taking a deep breath, she steeled herself for the fact he probably wouldn't make it—again. When it came to her swim meets, something always seemed to come up—an unscheduled conference, a last-minute call, an unexpected rush of work.

Getting focused again on the competition, Julie prepared for her race. Inside, though, she was angry—angry at her father's constant failure to take time off to watch her perform. He always seemed to have time to watch her brother play football, baseball, or whatever. He didn't make it to every game, but he went enough that he showed how important it was to him to watch Mark play.

Julie's dad had never shown up at one of her swim meets. He had promised to "see if I can make it" a half dozen times, but every time she scanned the crowd, she never saw his face. *I'm just not as important to him as Mark is*, she thought to herself, resisting that conclusion but making it nevertheless. What else was she to think? *If I were a boy, I bet he would watch me swim*. Anger built up inside of Julie. Anger was good; it made her swim faster. Her dad was just never there to see it.

Few things are as devastating to a child as the realization that her parents love a sibling more than they love her. Often it isn't so much that the parents love another more but rather that they love another more easily. For whatever reason, the ability to love the other child comes more naturally.

Children are not stupid. They can sense when this type of inequity exists. They can sense it even when the parent does not. Desperately they attempt to figure out what is wrong with them. The reasons they come up with can cause lifelong damage to self-esteem.

Parents have a variety of reasons for playing favorites with their children. Expectations of what they want each child to be are applied early, and each child is judged by a certain standard. Often the first and oldest child sets that standard. Temporarily the only child, the first child is accustomed to dealing mostly with adults from an early age and is often comfortable and deferential around adults. The children who follow are held accountable to emulate a situation that no longer exists in the family. Expectations are not met, and comments such as "Why can't you be more like your sister?" are the result.

It is said that opposites attract and equals repel. If you put magnets together one way, they quickly attract each other, but turn them around and try to push them together, and they push off in opposite directions. Sometimes friction is caused by the very traits in the adult that are present in the child. A willful mother will butt heads with a willful daughter. A sarcastic father will clash with a mouthy son.

In healthy relationships, differences are considered strengths and are used to build up each other. Each child in a family needs to be loved and accepted for who he or she is. Healthy families encourage their children's unique giftedness, and they practice love, acceptance, and forgiveness.

If you grew up in an unhealthy family, you may not have come to realize what a special person you are. Finding your specialness and truly feeling it will help you to reestablish your sense of self-worth. In chapter 12, I share how this can happen for you.

The Role Reverser

Adam had no joy in his voice. He answered my questions in a monotone, letting me know with every syllable how much he didn't want to be there. Adam's father, Frank, did want him to be there. Adam's mother, Judy, really didn't care, just as long as she didn't have to pay for it. She was just along for the ride.

Adam lived with his mother and saw his dad every other weekend. Frank had watched his happy, laughing son slowly fade. The parents had divorced when Adam was eleven—not an easy age. He was fourteen now, and Frank was convinced something was wrong. It wasn't just a phase Adam was going through.

Talking with Judy did no good at all, Frank explained. She had reacted violently and said he was trying to accuse her of being a bad mother. What did he know about what it was like to raise a child alone? All he had to do was take Adam a couple of days every other week. He had no idea how hard it was!

Frank had suggested having Adam start spending more time with him, but she blew up, saying the only way it would happen would be "over my dead body!"

At first Judy had been reluctant to take Adam to therapy at all, but then his grades started to suffer, and he was having trouble with kids at school. So she reluctantly agreed. Adam had no choice but to go.

For a while, I just spent time with Adam, finding out what his life was like. He didn't open up right away, but that really wasn't necessary for me to see what was going on. Just a few sessions with him and I knew what was wrong. When Adam's parents divorced, he had lost his mother and his father. They had ceased to exist.

For Judy, Adam was no longer her child. He became her companion, her confidant. She poured out on him how lonely she was feeling and how much Frank had hurt her. She told him that she didn't know what she would do if it weren't for him. He was all she had left in the world.

Adam cleaned the apartment whenever she was too tired, which was often. He cooked supper for them so she could unwind after work. He did the laundry, ran errands, and took care of her physical needs. Adam stopped being a child and became the parent to his mother. Their roles were all of a sudden reversed, and Adam felt the weight of adulthood before he was ready to shoulder it.

To make matters worse, Adam lost his dad at the same time. Whenever he went to Frank's for the weekend, it was one big party—movies, pizza, sporting events on television, and one-on-one games played outside. His dad didn't want to hear about the bad times; he just wanted his buddy back again. He wanted the Adam who played and laughed and didn't have a care in the world. Adam stopped having a father and found a pal instead.

The pressure to provide whatever his parents needed from him was too great. Adam had to reclaim his parents and his childhood. He had to stop being his mother's caregiver and his father's buddy all of the time.

Fortunately for Adam, his parents were able to take stock and realize what they had been doing. They hadn't meant for it to happen, but it had. Together they began to rebuild their lives and reassume their proper roles.

Often the most familiar use of the role reverser is in sexual situations, in which the parent, often the father, will put onto his daughter the role of lover—either physical or emotional or both. The daughter takes on the role of the wife, providing sexual companionship. When this abuse takes an emotional form, it is often very subtle. Parent and child may appear to the outsider as having a very loving relationship. People may comment on how close the two of them are.

Sexual relations between parent and child are called *incest*. The emotional side of such a relationship is called *emotional incest*, for the parent is using the child to fulfill his sexual needs, whether they be physical or emotional.

Role reversals can happen in other ways when the proper role within a relationship is switched. The parent becomes child. The child becomes parent. The parent becomes pal. The child becomes pal. When these roles are interfered with, needs are left unmet. A child needs to be a child, to have a parent to look to for guidance and example.

Children often enjoy reversing roles with their parents for a short time. The toddler brings Mommy her favorite blankie when she's taking a nap and tucks it lovingly under her chin like Mommy has done hundreds of times for her. The adolescent pals around with his dad over the weekend, just the two of them. These reversals provide children with a glimpse of what life will be like when they're older. While children enjoy these special moments on occasion, they shouldn't have to live that way, thrust into adulthood too early and denied childhood along the way.

The Empty Promiser

"Mom, can you drive me over to Jenny's house today? She's having some friends over and wanted me to come." Anna couldn't wait until she was old enough to get her driver's license so she wouldn't have to set herself up like this. But she'd secretly called just about everyone else she knew to see if she could get a ride over to Jenny's, without success. She was left with her last and most unreliable option—her mother.

"It's going to take forty minutes out of my day to drive you over there! If you want me to take you, you're just going to have to help me get some things done around here. If we get everything done, then I ought to be able to take you over there," her mother replied, looking up from the Saturday morning paper.

Reluctantly Anna got a list of chores from her mother and began tackling them one by one, even though her mother hadn't moved from the table and her coffee. Anna knew this was a risk. She could end up getting all of the chores done and then find out that this was only the first set of things her mother wanted her to do. If her mother really didn't want to take her, she'd find a way to postpone leaving the house until it wouldn't be worth going anyway. Still, there was no way to know that for sure, and Anna really did want to go to Jenny's. She figured she had a fifty-fifty chance. It depended upon how much stuff her mother wanted her to do and how little her mother wanted to get out of the house on a Saturday.

It was like this all the time. Her mother would say she'd do something, Anna would count on it, and then her mother would find a way not to do what she'd said.

As Anna worked around the house, she thought again to that all-important driver's license and the freedom it would bring. Of course, she'd still need to borrow her mother's car to go anywhere. But if she was lucky, her odds to have more freedom would go up.

Some people just give empty promises. They say they'll do something and they never do. Even if the other person fulfills some sort of imposed condition on their compliance, they find a way to renege at the last minute. This sort of behavior teaches children the lie that words don't really mean anything, that words can be used to manipulate other people to do what we want, and that we don't have to live up to our promises.

As adults, we know all of those lessons are false. We know that words do mean a great deal, that words should never be used to manipulate other people, and that we are expected to live up to our promises. The people around us expect that, and so does God. James says it this way in James 5:12: "Above all, my brothers, do not swear—not by heaven or by earth or by anything else. Let your 'Yes' be yes, and your 'No,' no, or you will be condemned."

When we fail to live up to our promises, we teach those around us that we don't value them enough to follow through.

The Wrath-of-God Abuser

"'Vengeance is mine,' saith the Lord, 'I will repay!'" The preacher thumped his hand on the podium and scanned the crowd. "'All have sinned and fallen short of the glory of God!' And that means all of you!" he screamed, pointing his finger randomly at the flock staring wide-eyed in front of him.

They knew the way he preached. "Fire and brimstone," they called it. They knew, and they liked it. He had been full of fire for the Lord each time. But lately he had begun to feel it was more smoke than fire. The raging passion in his gut for the Lord just wasn't there anymore. This would be the last time he preached for them, or for anyone. He just couldn't sustain the anger anymore.

Miserable, he didn't know what to do with himself. He had let down his family, let down his church, let down his God, and let down his father. A preacher who can't preach is miserable, and so he was. A man without a pulpit, he was lost and searching for who he really was when he stepped down from the stage.

He had always wanted to be a preacher, ever since he was a child watching his father deliver God's message to the enthralled crowd. He had idolized his dad. His dad was on fire for the Lord in everything he did, everywhere he went. His speech was filled with Scripture references. If he did anything wrong, his dad had a verse ready to call him into the Lord's condemnation.

He was constantly reminded of how unworthy he was, of how much he had sinned, of how far he had to go to earn God's love. He had learned the words and the Scriptures and how to tell others about their sinful lives. He stood in the pulpit himself and sounded the warning.

Now it was no longer enough. He had to stop shouting long enough to listen. He had to stop feeling sorry and start feeling forgiven. He had to stop viewing his heavenly Father as an awesome representation of his earthly one—full of righteous anger with no healing grace.

He had to realize that his whole life he had been hit over the head with the Bible. The words that had been written to bring him life instead convinced him of his death. His father had used a higher authority to rigidly enforce his own.

Slowly but surely, the preacher learned about love, forgiveness, and grace. He learned to love himself and those around him. He started haltingly to show forgiveness to himself when he failed and to extend grace to others when they failed too. The wrath of God was replaced by the love of God.

For those of you who did not grow up in a religious household, this type of emotional abuse may not apply. It involves the use of religion to belittle and control the behavior of others, and it is most effective in use with religious cults. Abusers of this sort present the idea that God is in league with them. You are to conform to what your abuser wants not only because he or she wants it but because *God* wants it too. The score instantly becomes two to one. The deck is stacked.

Whatever wrath-of-God abusers choose to do or say is backed by their use of the higher authority. They use Scripture and religious concepts to justify their abuse. This type of emotional abuse is often combined with the commander in chief, who takes ultimate orders from God himself.

Faith is a beautiful thing. Connecting yourself to the power of God can be an expanding experience. It can enable you to devote yourself to a worthy goal and provide you with motivation for acts of sacrifice and service. It can give meaning to your life and provide you with purpose. Faith should never be a bludgeon. God should never be used to diminish your sense of self. Religion should not strip away your self-worth; at its best it should contribute to your self-identity.

When actions such as hitting, throwing objects, making threats, and physically intimidating someone are used along with verbal abuse, the negative messages the verbal abuse delivers are reinforced, making for an abusive one-two punch. The words and the actions back each other up, creating powerful messages that need to be examined and countered. In chapter 12 we will explore how to do this. Powerful as they are, these messages can be replayed, both sight and sound, and put into proper perspective.

A Time to Heal

When emotionally abusive words and actions are combined, they reinforce each other, crushing one's sense of self. That is why it is so important to counter this abuse with affirming words and actions. In our relationships with others and ourselves, our words and actions are meant to build us up, not tear us down.

Here are the emotional abuse patterns we identified in this chapter:

- The commander in chief—who seeks to control all aspects of the relationship through an unhealthy use of authority (or perceived authority)
- The ventaholic—who constantly views actions by others as a threat and responds with bouts of rage

- The intimidator—who attempts to control the behavior of others through use of verbal or nonverbal threats
- The roller coaster—whose up-and-down mood swings decimate any sense of consistency and security
- The Dr. Jeykll and Mr. Hyde—whose public face is a lie and whose private face is abusive
- The illusionist—whose need to maintain an illusion of self denies his or her true nature
- The person who plays favorites—who fails to provide a level playing field in regard to love of others
- The role reverser—whose own sense of need causes basic relationships to be turned upside down
- The empty promiser—who takes advantage of the needs of others by giving a promise he or she never really intends to keep
- The wrath-of-God abuser—who uses the Bible to hit other people over the head

1. As you look over this list, are you able to identify people in your past or present who manifest these characteristics? Write their names and their relationship to you next to each type.
2. Which characteristics have had the most impact on your life? How have they impacted you?
3. Each one of these types taught you something about the world and how it works. Write down the things you learned that you believe are true.
4. Write down the things you learned that you believe are a lie.
5. What truths do you still find hard to believe today because of the abusive words and actions of others?

6. What negative messages do you still carry around today because of the abusive words and actions of others?

Seeing through the double blind of negative words and actions can be difficult. The fact that you are reading through this book, however, indicates that you are seeking to face the truth of your relationships and break through the bonds of your emotional abuse. While you mourn the truth of yesterday, don't forget to acknowledge the hope that lies in today and tomorrow. To help you do this, it's time to exercise your own words and actions.

Below, write down three strong affirmations about yourself. These can be something about who you are as a person, or they can be affirmations of your commitment to move beyond your abuse. As you write down your affirmations, you are countering your abuse with words.

My Statements of Personal Affirmation:

1. _____

2. _____

3. _____

Now, copy these statements of personal affirmation onto another piece of paper and place them in your purse or wallet. Or you can post them on a bathroom mirror, where you can see and repeat them to yourself every day. Every time you feel burdened to experience or relive the abuse you have endured, take out these words and remember your recommitment to hope. By repeating them to yourself daily, you can begin to rewrite those negative messages from your past.

6

Emotional Abuse through Neglect

> Missing in action—no end to the hope that someday a
> real relationship might happen. No end to the pain when
> it never does. No closure to a wound that stubbornly re-
> fuses to heal.

The emotional abuse talked about so far has been delivered
through the sarcastic remark, the scream of rage, the whine of
disappointment. We have seen it manifested in the absolute
rule of law, the up-and-down flux of moods, the thoughtless
actions of others. But there is another category of abuse that occurs without a word being spoken or a finger lifted. In fact, the
abuse comes about because no word is said or no action taken.

This is the emotional abuse that comes about through
indifference or inaction, through neglect—times when a
word should be said but isn't or an action should be taken
but is not forthcoming. As damaging as the other types of
emotional abuse are, it is the *absence* of the expected, of the
needed, that wounds.

With abuse through words or actions, what you expect
from your abuser is substituted with something else: a kind

word is replaced by a snide comment; a pat on the back is replaced by a slap across the face; a sense of belonging and security is replaced by a loss of safety and consistency.

Emotional abuse through indifference doesn't substitute any action for what might be expected from a loving, healthy relationship. Instead, there is only a gaping silence, a deaf ear, a turned back. When I was growing up, this was sometimes known as "the silent treatment." It was as total a withdrawal as possible of one person from another. For whatever reason, the abuser withholds relationship from the other person.

A child who is ignored may engage in attention-getting activities that are destined to produce negative results. While this might seem self-defeating, the real desire is for attention. Even if the response is negative, the parent has been forced to notice the child.

None of us likes to be ignored, treated as if we simply aren't important enough to notice. The person who has suffered this type of emotional abuse is saddled with the realization that his or her presence doesn't even cause a ripple in the world of the abuser. What is so damaging is that usually the abuser is someone from whom the person desperately wants to receive love and attention.

Children know and understand that the things with which adults concern themselves are important. When parents are involved in the life of their child, they communicate to the child that he or she is important. When parents fail to become involved, they communicate to the child a sense of rejection.

On a fundamental level, emotional abuse by neglect produces long-range damage. Children, especially infants, are hardwired to mature and grow in response to the environment—to the people—around them. It is imperative that infants experience a bonding relationship with parents through touch, eye contact, physical closeness, and auditory stimulation. These experiences cement positive brain development. According to Dr. Bruce D. Perry, an internationally recognized authority on brain development, "During the first three years of life, the human brain develops to 90 percent of adult size and puts in place the majority of systems and structures that will be responsible for all future emotional, behavioral, social, and psychological functioning during the rest of life."[1]

The tragedy of emotional abuse through neglect is that it can take place in homes where physical needs are met, even extravagantly met. Children need more than food on the table and a roof over their heads. They are designed to need a nurturing physical and emotional relationship with their parents. (Yes, parents, each gender gives something special and unique to a child. Children need both a mother and a father. Unfortunately, death or divorce often prevents children from having two parents. While it is possible to supplement the primary caregiver relationship with extended family and friends, children are very aware that something is missing. When that awareness is downplayed, marginalized, or rejected, children are further hurt.) When emotional needs are not met, children have difficulty progressing developmentally. It is as if they become "stuck" at a certain stage and progression is retarded. Emotionally neglected children are so hungry for emotional attachment that they may cling to strangers or other adults, displaying little natural caution around people they don't know.

In my work with eating disorders, I found a tie between disordered eating and childhood emotional neglect. Food or control of food becomes a substitute relationship for the one missing; it becomes friend, comforter, lover. This is often tied to unusual comforting behaviors, such as head banging, biting, scratching, or cutting. So fundamental is an emotional bond for connection, comfort, and stability that neglected children turn to inappropriate, damaging behaviors as a way to substitute and cope.

The MIA Parent

"He never wrote me, not once," Jan commented quietly, tears streaming down her face. "I kept hoping, like an idiot, every birthday, every Christmas, that I'd get something from him. I wasn't stupid enough to think he'd send a present, maybe just a card, something to show he remembered I was still alive."

Jan was thirty-six years old and had come to work with us at The Center because of her struggling marriage. She had already been divorced once and really wanted this second marriage to work. But Jan and her husband were having problems and were arguing a lot. Steve, Jan's husband, said she never trusted him. She always wanted to know where he was and with whom.

"She treats me like a child," he told me in counseling, "like she's afraid to let me out of her sight, afraid I might do something stupid."

As I talked to Jan, I realized she wasn't afraid for Steve, she was afraid for herself. Jan had been abandoned by her father at age six, though he had emotionally vacated the family years before that. Unhappy in his relationship with her mother, he had left the state and started a new life. Jan simply did not figure into it. At first he had used the excuse of the distance between them. That had worked when she was small. As years went by with minimal contact, Jan knew he refused to see her not because he couldn't or was too far away. He didn't have a relationship with her because he really didn't want to. She wasn't important to him now. Jan doubted she ever had been.

Jan's mother had tried to console her daughter by saying it was better for both of them that he was out of their lives forever. They could go on with their lives without him around to mess things up. The thirty-six-year-old completely agreed with her mother, but the six-year-old still longed for her daddy.

Distrustful and suspicious of men, Jan had a hard time with relationships. Convinced that any man she had a relationship with might leave her at any time, she always held some of herself back so she wouldn't be hurt so badly. Overly protective and controlling, she wasn't able to relax and trust within her relationships.

"Was I so bad?" she asked her father out loud during a session with Steve. Of course, her father wasn't physically there, but his actions permeated the room. "Why haven't you ever tried to see me?" A difficult question to an absent father. Finally, looking at me, she said, "The only time I'll get to see my father is at his funeral. While he's alive, he doesn't want to see me. When he's dead, he won't have a choice," Jan said angrily.

"I'm not your father," Steve said softly, taking her hand. "I won't leave you like he did." Steve rocked Jan in his arms as the six-year-old in his wife cried.

"Why?" Jan looked up at me again and asked. "What did I do that was so bad he had to go away?"

"Nothing," I told her. "It wasn't your fault he left. Jan, whatever his reasons were, it wasn't your fault."

Missing in action. No body recovered. No end to the hope that someday he might surface. No end to the pain when he never does. No closure to a wound that stubbornly refuses to heal completely.

In group sessions, when others would talk about an abusive father who would rant and rave or be so drunk he couldn't see straight, Jan would say, "At least he was there." For her it was better to be yelled at than to be forgotten. She needed to learn that neither was healthy.

Over the course of many years, I have seen this type of abuse most often in fathers. They leave their families and maintain marginal contact if any. They leave an unfinished chapter in their child's book of life. The ending never gets written. No matter what other relationships are formed afterward, the one with an absent father never has a resolution. There is no one to be angry with, no one to confront or accuse, and no one to whom you can say, "I forgive you, Dad."

Worst of all is the suspicion that the real reason Dad never came back is that you weren't special enough to him. Those who have been abandoned in this way often try to accomplish a great deal in their lives, hoping that if only they can do enough, their father will miraculously show up again, proud of his child at last, with some sort of plausible explanation for the years of abandonment.

Then comes that terrible moment when you have to come face-to-face with the fact that your father is a flawed, erring human being who had troubles of his own that caused him to leave. You have to be able to accept the fact that your presence wasn't enough to override the problems of the parent who left you, whether those problems stemmed from substance abuse, financial irresponsibility, intense marital conflict, or just plain selfishness. Coming to grips with this difficult reality means that you not only no longer have a father, but you also no longer are even able to have the image of the father you so wanted and needed him to be. Sometimes reality stinks, but fantasy is no way to live your life.

As mentioned in chapter 3, making yourself feel responsible for your abuse is an attempt to gain control over your situation. If you can say to yourself that your parent left because of something you did, there is always the chance he might come back if you change. To rid yourself of this false guilt, you will need to accept the fact that he might never come back, no matter what you do. You cannot continue to make yourself responsible for his actions, to blame yourself for his leaving. Once you rid yourself of that guilt, you can begin to rebuild your sense of self-worth.

The Distant Caregiver

Jesse had pretty much gotten used to being alone all the time. His mother never seemed to be around the apartment when he was. She usually had leftovers of some kind for him to heat up when he got home, but she was rarely around anymore. He was sixteen years old, and she felt he could take care of himself.

As soon as Jesse got out of school, he would head over to his job as a dishwasher at a local restaurant where he would work the dinner rush, getting home around nine o'clock. Sometimes his mom would be home, asleep in front of the television. At least three nights out of the week she would be gone, partying with friends. Sometimes she would come home late, sometimes not at all.

On the weekends Jesse's mom would have errands to run, and he would be out with his friends. They just never seemed to see each other much. Every once in a while she would say they really had to spend a night together, just the two of them, soon. But something always seemed to come up, either for her or for him.

Jesse had gotten used to not seeing much of his mom. He had grown up that way.

As our society changes, more and more kids are in Jesse's situation. Housed, fed, and clothed, their physical needs are met. They have a place to sleep, even if it is often alone. They never miss a meal, even if it's leftovers eaten in an empty house. They have shoes, jeans, and a winter coat, even if there doesn't ever seem to be anyone around to notice how they look.

Unlike MIA parents, distant caregivers aren't missing. Usually their children know exactly where they are or at least have a good idea. Distant caregivers aren't gone forever; they just show up in spurts.

As children grow, most experience the natural, normal process of establishing independence from their parents. In healthy relationships parents give their children the support and guidance needed to take their first steps, knowing that those steps will eventually lead away from the parent. But the parents also keep near for those times when their children turn around, notice how far they have gone, and come running back to reestablish their sense of belonging and identity.

When children are small, the steps are physical ones. As children grow, more and more of those steps are emotional. It is dangerous to think that because a child is physically able to be away from the parent, he or she is well equipped to be emotionally apart as well.

In distant-caregiver abuse, parents prematurely withdraw themselves emotionally from their child. They no longer enmesh themselves in their child's emotional framework. This may be because of indifference or because of an overt decision to force the child to go it alone. Whatever the reason, such action is abusive, for it denies children the emotional anchor from which they can explore their own identity. Sometimes this is a pattern of behavior that remains consistent from the child's infancy. Parents who grew up without a deep emotional attachment may have difficulty understanding or being able to establish proper emotional attachment with their own children.

The Emotionally Detached Parent

Tina came to The Center because she was compulsively overeating, had difficulty establishing relationships, and was incessantly scratching herself. At twenty-eight years old, she was over three hundred pounds and covered with self-induced sores. Angry and defensive, Tina found it hard to be friends with other people, let alone establish a romantic relationship. High school had been a nightmare, and Tina thought that once she got out into the working world things would be better. She was intelligent and able to perform a variety of tasks, but she hadn't anticipated how her expanding weight would hamper her ability to get better-paying jobs. It made her angry to think other people looked down on her because of her size. The angrier she got, the more she ate. The larger she became, the more problems she had on the job and with other people.

The more problems she had, the more she picked at her skin and never-healing sores. When Tina started talking about ending her life, her sisters intervened and arranged for her to come to work with me.

With a few variations, Tina's story was hauntingly familiar. Tina was the oldest of three girls born to a working-class family. Her parents were owners of a small business that was the livelihood of the whole family, and the whole family was expected to make sacrifices for it to be successful. Tina was asked to sacrifice a relationship with her mother and father, who farmed her out to relatives, neighbors, and disinterested teenage babysitters, in order to keep the business going. When her parents were home, they were exhausted, distracted, short-tempered, and distant. Their minds were on the business. The business thrived; Tina did not.

Tina was an only child until age seven, when her sister was born, followed by the youngest sister two years later. It wasn't long before Tina was acting as caregiver to her younger sisters. She learned to cook and clean, get her sisters and herself to school, help with their homework, and manage the house. They always had food to eat and clothes to wear. The business, after all, was doing great. It was so successful, in fact, that Tina's parents opened a second store and started the cycle all over again.

Tina found she loved to cook, so her mother ceded control of the kitchen over to Tina fairly early. Tina loved the warmth of the kitchen and the comforting smells of the food. She also found a solace for the emotional void in her life. Food brought her the admiration of her sisters, the gratitude of her mother, the notice of her father, and comfort for her soul. She put on weight at adolescence and just kept going.

The scratching started shortly after, during her sophomore year in high school, when her weight blossomed and her popularity withered.

Wanting to end her life was not so much a statement of despair as anger. Tina threatened to end her life out of rage that she had never really been allowed to live it. She had never been allowed to be a child. She had never been allowed to expect or even demand attention, affection, and validation from her too-busy parents.

While Tina's parents would later protest that they had concentrated so much on the business because of her, Tina knew that was not true. The truth was they enjoyed the status and success of the business. They found it more rewarding to be shop owners than parents. Tina also needed to come to terms with her own truth—about her anger and motivations to continue with her destructive eating patterns and scratching behaviors. Tina needed to learn that even though she never felt loved as a child, it was possible to love herself as an adult.

Because seeking the acceptance and approval of those we look to for love and relationship comes naturally, it is difficult not to take our feelings of worth from them. Two reasons can be given for the absence of acceptance and approval: either they are being wrongly withheld or the source of acceptance and approval is absent. In either case, gaining that acceptance and approval is difficult at best.

Is the answer then to give up trying to gain acceptance and approval completely, since it seems to be a lost cause either way? No. The answer is to open your eyes and see that there are other places to gain the acceptance and approval you need. The answer is to seek out those who won't withhold their acceptance and approval and who will maintain relationship with you and not leave. The answer is to learn to make wise choices about whom you seek approval from and to look for support from family, friends, or the church of your choice.

A Time to Heal

This chapter is the smallest in this section, but its impact is huge. Here are the types again from the chapter:

- The MIA parent—who emotionally and physically abandons his or her responsibility as a parent
- The distant caregiver—who is physically present but emotionally distant and withdrawn from his or her children
- The emotionally detached parent—who provides for his or her children in every way except for emotional bonding and attachment

1. Did you grow up in a home with both parents? If so, were you closer to one than the other? Why?
2. Did you grow up in a single-parent household? Who did you live with the majority of the time?
3. Was your other parent involved in your life? How much?
4. Did you grow up with a parent who was emotionally detached from you? Do you remember when you first noticed this detachment?
5. What reason did you give yourself for this detachment? Did you blame yourself for the distance between the two of you?

6. What were the most important things to your father as you were growing up?

7. What were the most important things to your mother as you were growing up?

8. Did you grow up feeling you weren't as important as these things were to one or both of your parents?

9. Do you remember wishing you were as important as these things were?

10. How often do you remember being apart from your parents in relation to each of these important things?

11. What strategies did you develop as a child to deal with the physical or emotional abandonment of one or both of your parents?

12. Are those strategies still present in your life today? How are they manifested?

13. Are these lingering strategies a positive or a negative in your life? Please explain.

14. If you are a parent, what steps have you taken to remain emotionally close and accessible to your children?

15. How has the emotional distance or withdrawal from one or both parents affected your understanding of and relationship with God?

16. When you think about God in your own life, do you consider him to be present but distant?

17. Does that cause you pain or comfort? Why?

No matter how we feel, the truth is that God does not abandon us, not even for a moment. Even with all he is doing in this world and in the spiritual realm, he does not take a moment off. Psalm 121:2–3 says, "My help comes from the LORD, the Maker of heaven and earth. He will not let your foot slip—he who watches over you will not slumber." God is right with you, always. He is not subject to weakness or distraction or apathy. He loves you deeply, passionately, and continually.

18. Read Matthew 6:25–34, from the Sermon on the Mount. What does this passage reveal about God's care and concern for you?

19. Based on this passage, do you believe you are important to God?

20. Do you believe that God values you highly? Do you believe and yet still have doubts?

21. What are two positive steps you can take today to put those doubts behind you?

Though neglect or abandonment has depleted your emotional life, it is possible to restore emotional strength. You do so by believing and internalizing the following truths:

I have value because God has given it to me.

Through the mistreatment of others, I have developed a faulty sense of self. I accept this truth and am learning more about who I really am and who I am meant to be every day.

My self-respect and innate dignity are a gift from God that can never be taken away.

I am learning to treat myself with dignity and respect, even if others have not done so in the past.

I am no longer a victim. Today I celebrate being a victor!

7

Spiritual Abuse

The Bible as Bludgeon

Spiritual abuse carries its own unique watermarks. Clothed in religiosity, they can be difficult to discern at first, but they always end up showing their true colors.

Martin entered the church building quietly, glancing around to see if anyone noticed. It was late afternoon, and though there were a few scattered cars in the parking lot, he didn't see anyone as he made his way inside. He stopped just inside the foyer to collect his thoughts, again going over in his mind what he was going to say. Wiping the sweat from his upper lip, he took a deep breath and walked down the hallway to the church offices.

The building felt so different on a Tuesday. On Sunday morning, it was crowded with friends and fellow believers happy to see one another and eager to receive a blessing from the pastor. He rarely went into this part of the church, where there were offices for senior staff. These were the halls of power, and Martin felt sorely out of place. Instead of going into the large sanctuary where it was easy to be swallowed up in anonymity, he was headed into the pastor's private study. He felt alone and exposed, with no crowd for camouflage.

Coming into the reception area, Joan, the secretary, looked up while on the phone and motioned for him to have a seat along the wall. She appeared to be in a lengthy discussion about the upcoming Easter event. Martin couldn't tell who she was speaking to, but he didn't want to bother her, so he kept as quiet as possible. There were a few church publications out on the small table near his chair. Without anything to do but worry prior to the meeting, he leafed through them. With a twinge of annoyance, he recognized them as things he'd already seen, having received them in his church bulletins over the past month or so. Disappointed, he again took a seat.

After a couple more minutes, it sounded like Joan was wrapping up her phone call, and he heard her say, "Oh, yes, Martin is here to see you." With a jolt, he realized she'd been talking to the pastor, who was now aware he'd arrived. His stomach began to turn, and he self-consciously wiped a fresh round of sweat from around his mouth.

Joan hung up the phone and said, "I'll take you back. Pastor Roberts can see you now." She walked past him and opened the door to the inner offices. Martin followed, feeling like a scared kid about to see the doctor.

Pastor Roberts opened the door to his office just as he and Joan arrived. Smiling broadly, he greeted Martin with a loud voice and praised God for his safe arrival. Joan, without a word, melted back through the doorway into the reception area. Martin was now alone with Pastor Roberts.

In so many ways, the damage of emotional abuse is magnified when a disparity of position exists between the abuser and the victim. The more authority or control an abuser has over his or her victim, the greater the damage that can be inflicted. If you're driving in your car and another driver gets mad and gestures at you, it might take you several hours to get over the incident. It will bother you, but you'll be able to put it into perspective. However, if a parent berates you loudly for something you've done, it's going to take longer to put that incident into perspective, if you can at all. Why? Because the driver in the car really doesn't have any authority or control over you beyond what you give him or her. A parent, on the other hand, has a great deal of authority and control over you, your actions, and how you view yourself.

Imagine, then, the damage that can be inflicted when the person with control and authority over you is God himself.

Pastor Roberts put his arm around Martin's shoulders and led him to a set of chairs at the side of his desk. After they sat down, the pastor prayed a quick, fervent prayer that he would be granted wisdom and discernment in the conversation to follow. Martin said, "Amen," his head spinning.

Martin increasingly felt like he just wanted to say what he had to say and get it over with, but Pastor Roberts began to ask about how his wife, Connie, was doing and how things were going at home.

"And how's your boy—Jeff, isn't it? Won't he be turning eight soon?" Martin was always amazed at how the pastor could keep everyone straight in his mind with such a large congregation. Without realizing it, he found himself verbalizing the thought.

"Well," Pastor Roberts replied, "I consider every one of you to be given to me by God, to pastor, to lead, and to guide. Why, it says in John 10, verses 2–4, that I am to know my sheep by name and to call them out of this world. I take that commandment very seriously. Now, as your shepherd, Martin, how can I lead you today?" His eyes looked intently at Martin with care and concern.

"Actually, um, I've got a decision to make fairly soon about a promotion at work. Connie and I talked about it and decided we needed some guidance since it means moving to Cleveland, Ohio." There, he'd said it. Now all he had to do was wait for Pastor Roberts's reaction.

In spiritual abuse, people with authority and control over you present themselves as having divine authority. They usurp God's authority and exert power and control over you—sometimes with the very best of motives, often with warped personal intentions. They aren't God but position themselves as his spokesperson in and for your life. They use the Bible as a bludgeon to coerce you into giving up your own free will and turning it over to their personal revelation of what's "best" for you. Too often, what's "best" for you translates ultimately into what's best for them. Like any emotional abuser, they seek to control your thoughts, attitudes, and actions for their benefit so they can feel better about their own life and about themselves.

"Tell me why you think this move is a good idea," Pastor Roberts said after several moments of silence. His expression was now mainly one of concern.

"I've really thought about it," Martin began slowly before picking up speed. "It's a promotion within the company, something I've been working toward for four years. It'll mean a significant increase in salary. Besides, I've got two really good friends from college who live just outside of Cleveland. They say the economy is booming there right now and have already promised to help us with the move, getting situated in schools, that sort of thing." He paused before continuing, "We've prayed about it a lot, Connie and I. We just want to make sure it's God's will."

Pastor Roberts said nothing.

"That's why we thought I should come and talk to you," Martin said into the awkward silence, "to receive your blessing for this move." Martin ended on a more hopeful note than he felt. Pastor Roberts didn't look enthusiastic.

Throughout the ages, spiritually abusive movements have come and gone on the religious scene. They generally are started by charismatic, powerful leaders who, in a short period of time, gather relatively large numbers of followers. These leaders are decisive and persuasive, tapping into a strongly felt need for order and security. Pledging to completely change a person's life, they make faith the currency and God the guarantor of their promises.

Just as there are certain specific types of emotional abuse, spiritual abuse carries its own unique watermarks. Clothed in religiosity, they can be difficult to discern at first, but they always end up showing their true colors. The sooner a person can recognize their true nature, the better.

Types of Spiritual Abuse

Abuse of Control

Spiritually abusive leaders, churches, and organizations have, at their core, an obsessive need to control the thoughts and actions of their followers. The independent thoughts and actions of their followers are viewed as threatening. Often what they ask of their followers is difficult, leading to natural rebellion. Only by controlling their followers' thoughts and actions can these organizations gain and maintain compliance.

I remember one such group (whose influence has waned significantly over the years) who required every believer to have an accountability partner. This was someone of the same gender who was appointed by the organization, not someone chosen by the person. The follower was required to share every aspect of his or her life with the accountability partner, who would then pass judgment, in essence giving a spiritual thumbs-up or thumbs-down. For those who were married, this included a requirement to share intimate, personal details of their married life with this appointed accountability partner.

As Christians and simply as people, we recognize the special, private, and intimate relationship between spouses. There are aspects of our personal lives and married lives that we simply should not be required to share with another person, especially another person who has been appointed for us. This goes against the grain. I remember being shocked at such an invasive requirement. Everything I knew about God and Scripture spoke against it. The couple who shared their experiences after leaving this church could only shake their heads and explain that they had felt their natural reticence was a sign of spiritual rebellion. In order to "prove" their love and devotion to God, they breached their marital relationship and allowed the scrutiny and control of others, even into this most intimate and private aspect of their lives.

I have heard of leaders and churches that choose marital partners for their members. Sadly, the news is periodically filled with accounts of teenagers and young adults who have been married against their will or coerced into sexual relationships with other followers at the direction of their leader or leaders. We often associate this kind of behavior with those churches or organizations we label as cults. However, I have known of people who were directed by their churches to divorce their current spouse so they could marry someone else within the church. I have also heard of leaders and churches that demanded such obedience from followers that they decided who the followers were to marry, where they were to live, where their children were to go to school, what activities they were to take part in, and what family and friends they were to associate with. This level of control over personal and private decisions is a hallmark of a spiritually abusive organization.

Abuse of Money

Emotionally abusive people generally engage in abusive behaviors for their own personal benefit. The control they exert over others has some sort of benefit in their lives, from reducing fear to enhancing feelings of personal superiority to insuring personal comfort, pleasure, or satisfaction. For spiritually abusive people and organizations, one of the primary areas of control is over the followers' finances. Money, after all, is a substitute for and provider of power. The more money a leader or organization brings in, the more power that person or organization has to affect their surroundings.

Gaining money means power. Giving money means surrender. After all, except for taxes, anything else we give our money to really is a personal choice. From where we live to what we eat to what we wear, we make individual decisions even about basic needs. Only the government can garnish wages; churches and religious organizations cannot. Any money they receive comes from the voluntary actions of their followers or members. This puts these churches and organizations in a somewhat precarious position: they must persuade people to give. But even though their position is precarious, it is also very powerful. Since time immemorial, churches and religious organizations have equated riches with righteousness. This powerful connection has been used incredibly effectively over the ages as a way to milk followers of money. This "milk money" has been used for a great deal of good and noble causes; it has also padded the nest of more than a few pastoral peacocks.

Abuse of Self

In order to gain control over another person, the emotional abuser sets up a pattern of undermining that person's sense of self. This makes the person easier to control. This tactic is in full force in a spiritually abusive church or organization. For these, the "bully pulpit" is just that—a place to berate, belittle, and spiritually batter people into giving up control of their own lives and ceding that control to another.

Within these types of churches, the tone of preaching and teaching is one of extreme negativity. The followers are made to feel bad, worthless, and unworthy. Messages are filled with guilt and shame. Every sin is scrutinized, and an endless spotlight is placed upon the ideas and actions of the follower, always through a negative filter. Even so-called good actions are called into question because they aren't good enough. Any slip is proof of unworthiness. At some point, the followers no longer feel able to judge the rightness or wrongness of an action or thought and must go to others within the organization to interpret their spiritual compass.

With no clear vision of who they are, or convinced of how bad they are, people will do just about anything for relief and salvation. At that point, they are imminently controllable by the powers that be, which is right where the spiritually abusive leader or organization wants them.

Abuse of Relationship

Christianity, while a religion, is really a relationship. It is a relationship with Jesus Christ. Spiritually abusive leaders, churches, and organizations are not interested in their followers having a personal, individual relationship with Jesus Christ. Rather, they always want to act as the intercessor between God and follower. This way they can determine the veracity of the relationship, matching it up with their own template of what a "true relationship" with God and Christ looks like.

It can be difficult to pinpoint something as ethereal as a relationship. So much of a relationship is about thoughts and feelings, which can be notoriously easy to hide and hard to judge. For the spiritually abusive, therefore, another measurement must be used to determine how committed, sincere, or obedient followers are. This is where spiritual works come into play. Spiritual works are the physical actions followers take that indicate how "real" their relationship is. Spiritually abusive leaders, churches, and organizations have elaborate rules and requirements that followers must meet to prove their depth of relationship and devotion to the cause.

The couple I spoke about before, who left a spiritually abusive church, was required to go out several nights a week and engage in evangelistic efforts for the church. They had to do this even though they had small children at home. The church appointed other members to babysit their children so they could be off doing what the church deemed appropriate for them in the evenings and on weekends. How often they were away from home, devoting themselves to the "work of the church," equated to how deeply committed and how healthy their relationship with God was. They told me this aspect of their experience is what eventually drove them to fall away. In the end, they could not justify the neglect and abandonment of their children any further. They faced a decision of either losing their faith or losing their children.

This is the type of choice that spiritually abusive leaders, churches, and organizations present their followers. There are no nuances, no shades of gray. Things are either totally right or totally wrong, with the church standing in the position of right.

Abuse of Promise

The Bible is full, from end to end, of the promises of God: his promises to be faithful, steadfast in love, patient, and compassionate. Every statement of God is a promise, for he does not lie, nor does he go back on his word. Just as the emotionally abusive person will use threats and promises—the proverbial stick and carrot—to maintain control over others, so too do spiritually abusive leaders, churches, and organizations. While they work hard to convince the follower of his or her own unrighteousness, they will often tie this to lavish promises of what following will bring. There's just one catch—all of the promises can come only if the person has enough faith.

Often others in the church will give testimony of how they were able to save their marriage, escape from addiction, be healed from sickness, or become financially successful because of the faith they gained by being with the church. All these good things are presented as proof of the power of membership, of adhering to the tenets and doctrines of the organization. They are presented as spiritual perks, similar to the kind of promotion done in multilevel marketing schemes. If you work hard within the system, look at all the "blessings" you'll receive. If your spouse ends up leaving you after all, if you need to enter into treatment instead of being miraculously healed of an addiction or illness, or if your business is still struggling, it's all your fault. You didn't have enough faith in God or the organization, so you failed. There's still something wrong with you, so you need to work harder, pray harder, give more, and surrender more.

The spiritually abusive organization presents itself as the avenue for the follower to unlock the "promise equation": "If I only do _____, then God will give me _____." With this kind of powerful equation, the follower is motivated to continue with those who constantly dangle in front of him or her what they say is the key to it all. Blessings from God, then, come down not to grace but to works—works determined by the organization.

Abuse of Vision

One of the most pervasive aspects of spiritually abusive leaders (for it all comes down to the leaders in the end) is this idea of vision. God's Spirit works within the lives of his people, guiding and directing them to recognize, understand, and interpret the vision God has for them. God, in his wisdom, gave his Spirit to each person as a personal seal of salvation. This is the essence of God's relationship with his people—deeply personal, with high value placed on the uniqueness of each person and a vision for that person as unique as the individual.

I have two wonderful boys at home. Each one is a unique person, with characteristics and traits that couldn't be farther from the other. My boys are not clones of each other. As such, each of them needs to be interacted with in a special way. There is no "one size fits all" for my kids. Even if the action or idea I need to convey to one of them is the same as to the other, my approach, tone, and words may be completely different. I understand each of them and know what it takes to speak to their hearts individually. Now, I'm just an average man and father. If I understand this in my limited experience, how much more does God understand this with all of us, his children? God, through his Spirit, speaks to our hearts individually and uniquely.

Spiritually abusive leaders rob the follower of his or her individuality to God. They blind a person's spiritual vision so he or she is no longer able to see the unique gifts, mission, and future God has in mind. God's vision for his or her life is crowded out with the forceful vision of the organization. In their obsessive need for control, spiritually abusive leaders want to determine what the follower's gifts are—generally whatever task or job they need filled at the time. They want to determine what the follower's mission in life is—to make sure it coincides with their mission. They want to determine what the follower's future will look like—to ensure they maintain control over him or her in that future.

Jeremiah 29:11—the theme verse, by the way, of The Center—says, "'For I know the plans I have for you,' declares the LORD, 'plans to prosper you and not to harm you, plans to give you hope and a future.'" Instead of living out that promise, spiritually abusive leaders want to substitute the Great "I" of this verse with their own "I," projecting their small and petty desires onto God.

Sitting back in his chair, Pastor Roberts spoke in deep, even tones. "I'm disappointed in you, Martin. I'm disappointed that you could even think of taking your family away from this church, especially after all we've done for you. I thought by now you'd be spiritually stronger."

"Oh, I am!" Martin protested, leaning forward in his chair. "I've listened to everything you've said. I've read all the church bulletins and publications. Connie and I, we read our Bible and pray daily. Since coming here, our lives have just been so blessed!"

"Then how could you even think about leaving? Why don't we take a look at the reasons you just now gave me for this move." As he said this, those reasons fled into the back corners of Martin's mind.

Pastor Roberts reached out his hand and began counting off with his finger. "The very first reason was all about pride. Proverbs 16:18 says pride goes before destruction and a haughty spirit before a fall. Have you considered, Martin, that you want this move because you're being prideful about the promotion?"

"Well, I have been working very hard for the last four years to get it." Martin could feel himself becoming defensive, but he cautioned himself against showing any hint to the pastor.

"If you took this promotion, it wouldn't be about your own efforts. It would be God working through you. James 1:17 clearly says that every good and perfect gift comes from God, not through our own efforts!" The pastor's voice echoed in the office.

"So you're saying this promotion is a gift from God? Then I should take it!" Martin couldn't quite see the logic, but it got him to where he wanted to go—Cleveland.

"By no means," the pastor said. "Leaving this church would not bring glory to God. Just being considered for the promotion, and thereby giving God glory through your employment, is sufficient. The fact of the promotion is enough. God does not expect you to actually take your family and leave. It's enough that you've brought God glory through this. However, you must decline the promotion so you and your family can stay here."

That seemed to bring the discussion to a close as far as Pastor Roberts was concerned. However, he probably could tell from Martin's expression that he still had doubts. So he continued, "If that's not clear enough for you, Martin, consider your other reasons. Do you remember the second thing you mentioned?"

Martin couldn't remember the order of things and didn't want to be wrong, so he remained silent.

"You talked about the money. Greed, Martin. Greed was your second reason for leaving this church. First Timothy 6, verse 10, specifically speaks to you." Pastor Roberts got up from his chair and retrieved his open Bible from the desk. Flipping toward the back of the book, he found the verse he was looking for. "Listen, Martin. It says, 'For the love of money is a root of all kinds of evil. Some people, eager for money, have wandered from the faith and pierced themselves with many griefs.' Martin, that could be you! You cannot allow your love of money to sway you into leaving!" Martin could hear the anguish in Pastor Roberts's voice.

"But Connie and I always tithe. You know we do!"

"Your heart still harbors greed and love of money, Martin. Otherwise you wouldn't have revealed the real reason—you are placing money over God. You must stay here; you're not yet spiritually mature."

"Really, it's not about the money. Although it would be nice to have a little bit more at the end of each month. I mean, the kids are growing up, and we haven't saved anything for college." Martin knew his excuses sounded feeble, but he just couldn't seem to keep up with all the pastor's objections.

"And what about the last reason you gave?" Pastor Roberts shook his head.

"You mean my buddies from college?" Martin had no idea what could be wrong with that. The pastor didn't even know Mike and Ron.

"They're not believers, are they?"

"Well, Mike's a Lutheran, and Ron goes to a community church."

"They're not believers, Martin. They're not affiliated with this church. We don't have a mission work yet in Cleveland. You cannot venture out without a true church home to belong to. Perhaps in a couple of years, when you're stronger, you might be ready to be part of a mission work to Cleveland."

"But the promotion is now! If I say no, I might not get another chance!"

"What do you care more about, Martin? God or your job? You've got a lot to learn. There is still sin in your life that needs to be addressed. No, you're not going anywhere. And I expect you and Connie to increase your tithe by twenty percent, beginning this Sunday. Money is obviously an area you need to bring under God's control."

With that, Martin was dismissed.

He walked out of the office, past Joan, without even saying good-bye. She was busy at her desk and barely noticed his leaving.

Getting into his car, he felt nauseated. He really wanted that promotion to Cleveland. A verse sprang to his mind, one that Pastor Roberts had preached on two Sundays ago. He couldn't remember where it was found, but it went something like, "What good is it for a man to gain the whole world, and yet lose or forfeit his very self?" Sitting quietly in the car, Martin realized he may have already done so.

This isn't the kind of religious life God wants us to live. This isn't why Christ died, for us to be enslaved by religious leaders. In fact, it was against this very evil behavior that Christ fought. As the body of Christ, we must continue fighting against this kind of spiritual abuse today.

What God Has to Say

Controlling, self-seeking, greedy, and oppressive spiritual leaders, churches, and organizations are nothing new, really. The delivery system may be new—television and the Internet—but the substance is the same: people using religion to gain control over others and therefore satisfy their own needs. As Solomon said in Ecclesiastes 1:9, "What has been will be again, what has been done will be done again; there is nothing new under the sun." Because this problem has been with us for a while now, there has been ample opportunity for God to weigh in on the matter. And when he has weighed in, he's come down pretty hard.

About Spiritual Abuse

From the beginning, God set apart those who would shepherd his flock. This visual picture was immediately recognizable and understandable to his people. Now, I don't have a herd of sheep in my backyard, but I can still understand how this metaphor works. God has always meant for the leaders of his church to have the welfare of the flock as paramount. He is therefore not pleased when spiritual leaders fail to faithfully execute their God-given duties.

In the book of Jeremiah, God indicted the failed shepherds of Israel, counting them responsible for leading the people astray. Because of their failed leadership, the people deviated off the path God set for them and wandered into idolatry and sin. This brought about implementation of the curses God had included in his covenant with his people. God had told them they would wind up in captivity if they lived in sin. This promise was fulfilled in the days of Jeremiah, when Judah was carted off into Babylonian captivity.

> "Woe to the shepherds who are destroying and scattering the sheep of my pasture!" declares the LORD. Therefore this is what the LORD, the God of Israel, says to the shepherds who tend my people: "Because you have scattered my flock and driven them away and have not bestowed care on them, I will bestow punishment on you for the evil you have done," declares the LORD.
>
> Jeremiah 23:1–2

Some of the most vivid condemnations of spiritual abuse have come from the mouth of Jesus himself. In unflattering terms he consistently condemned false teachers and oppressive religious leaders. He referred to them as a "brood of vipers" (Matt. 3:7), as "blind guides" (15:14; 23:16, 24), and as "hypocrites" all through the book of Matthew, especially in chapters 23 and 24. Jesus condemned them for doing their good deeds for show (6:2), praying for show (6:5), and fasting for show (6:16). He exposed their "evil intent" as they sought to trap him (22:18).

In Matthew 23, Jesus gave an extended, impassioned speech against the spiritual abuse perpetrated by these oppressive and false leaders:

- He condemned them for piling heavy burdens on the people while not lifting a finger to help (vv. 1–4).
- He condemned them for prideful motives and conducting their leadership for the notice and praise of people instead of God (vv. 5–7).
- He condemned them for taking on positions of authority for power and self-aggrandizement instead of for good (vv. 8–11).
- He condemned them for barring entrance to the kingdom of heaven (v. 13).
- He condemned them for zealously teaching a false doctrine to others (v. 15).
- He condemned them for placing more value on the offering than on the foundation of sacrifice (vv. 16–22).
- He condemned them for adhering to the letter of the law while completely disregarding the intent—they strained out a gnat to swallow a camel (vv. 23–24).
- He condemned them for putting on a polished appearance while allowing sin to corrupt their very selves (vv. 25–28).

- He condemned them for denying their own abusive histories (vv. 29–32).

As I think back in just my own lifetime of the many false teachers and leaders who have burst forth on the religious scene only to be crushed under the weight of their own misdeeds, I find that these words of Jesus ring true. Here is what I take out of Matthew 23:

- As a follower of Christ, I am to scrupulously avoid leaders who set up a double standard, one for themselves and one for everyone else.
- I must watch out for leaders whose motivations are public praise and selfish ambition. I must gauge their attitudes and actions for true Christlike humility.
- I am to guard against false teachings that divert me from finding and following God's true path for my life. I do this by taking responsibility for my own relationship with God and understanding his Word and his will for my life.
- I am to be alert to how my leaders deal with the entire subject of money and what weight and importance is given to material wealth and gain.
- I am to evaluate the role of grace versus works in my leaders. I am to determine if grace is being drowned out by a constant drumbeat of works, works, and more works, all to the cadence of perfectionism.
- I am to look for transparency, honesty, confession, and accountability in my leaders. If they do not exhibit these qualities, they are not fit to lead God's people.

About True Leadership

Scripture does not just describe false leadership; it also highlights what true leadership is all about. Earlier, in the Jeremiah 23 passage, we read of God's condemnation of false shepherds in verses 1 and 2. If we go on to read verse 4, it explains what good shepherds are supposed to do: "'I will place shepherds over them who will tend them, and they will no longer be afraid or terrified, nor will any be missing,' declares the LORD." True shepherds care for their flocks. They keep them safe and secure. They go after any who stray.

Ultimately, leaders must have the heart of Jesus, which means having a servant's heart. This is one of God's paradoxes: the person who wants to be a leader must become a servant to do so. This goes against our very nature. Jesus, knowing that, said in Luke 22:25–26: "The kings of the Gentiles lord it over them; and those who exercise authority over them call themselves Benefactors. But you are not to be like that. Instead, the greatest among you should be like the youngest, and the one who rules like the one who serves." After an argument arose among his disciples about who was going to be the greatest in the kingdom, Jesus told them very succinctly, "If anyone wants to be first, he must be the very last, and the servant of all" (Mark 9:35).

As with many other things Jesus said to the disciples and to us, sometimes we need an example in order to really understand the meaning. Right before Jesus was betrayed, he provided such an example: he washed the feet of the disciples. I'm not sure that in our antiseptic lives today we have a true picture of what washing feet back then meant. But in a world without sanitary systems, without asphalt paving and concrete, without medical technology—a world awash with dust, dirt, disease, and dung—washing feet was not an upper-tier job. It was obviously the task of a servant. The closest comparison I can make to it today, perhaps, is the person who cleans airport restrooms. In any case, partially disrobing in order to wash someone's feet was nowhere near the job description of a leader. Yet Jesus did so to prove a very important point. In John 13:12–15, he explained why he did this inexplicable act:

> When he had finished washing their feet, he put on his clothes and returned to his place. "Do you understand what I have done for you?" he asked them. "You call me 'Teacher' and 'Lord,' and rightly so, for that is what I am. Now that I, your Lord and Teacher, have washed your feet, you also should wash one another's feet. I have set you an example that you should do as I have done for you."

Leaders should have a servant's heart—humble, contrite, and full of grace. This is true biblical leadership.

About True Religion

Spiritually abusive churches and organizations are often consumed with growth for growth's sake. This is because growth equates to money, which equates to power. This power is then used to acquire more. Nothing could be further from God's definition of true religion, which James records for us in James 1:27: "Religion that God our Father accepts as pure and faultless is this: to look after widows and orphans in their distress and to keep oneself from being polluted by the world." There's nothing in there about perfect adherence to doctrines or demands to engage in grand projects and schemes. Instead, it's pretty simple—help others and watch yourself.

God hates oppression. I find this to be a particularly comforting aspect of his character. Only someone with power, control, and authority over you can oppress you. Otherwise you can just walk away. God has the ultimate power, control, and authority over my life. If he wanted to oppress me, he could do so second to none. Yet it is not in his nature to oppress. Instead, his heart goes out to the orphan, the fatherless, the widow, and the powerless people in the world. The book of Psalms is full of God's care and concern for the oppressed.

It is therefore doubly cruel when those who purport to be speaking for God do the very thing God hates—oppress their followers. This is one of the reasons Jesus spoke out so vehemently against the religious leaders of his day. Our Christian life is to be one marked by freedom, by relief from oppression, and by the constant encouragement and uplifting presence of the Holy Spirit. Spiritually abusive environments use religion to shackle, enslave, beat down, manipulate, and control. Spiritually abusive environments belittle, badger, humiliate, and condemn. All this is done to strip the follower of his or her individual relationship with God and substitute a spiritually abusive relationship with the leader, church, or organization.

This kind of slavery is not what Christ died for. As you're reading through this chapter, if you recognize this kind of enslavement in your past or present, it's time to break free.

Finding Your Spiritual Balance

If you have suffered the spirit-crushing weight of emotional abuse, you may find yourself especially susceptible to spiritually abusive environments. This is because the atmosphere of diminished sense of self, condemnation, black-and-white extremes, and forcefulness is familiar territory. If you were emotionally abused in the past, you may gravitate toward emotionally abusive relationships in the present and in the future. This includes your spiritual relationship with God. If you feel you are worthless, incompetent, damaged, and guilty due to the messages of emotional abuse, the underlying themes of a spiritually abusive environment will hit all the right chords. Those chords are in harmony with your abusive past.

This harmony, however, is a cacophony of lies. You need to reject it so you can hear the true "music of the spheres," as the beautiful hymn "This Is My Father's World" says. Zephaniah 3:17 speaks of a completely different type of music, a song sung to you by God himself: "The LORD your God is with you, he is mighty to save. He will take great delight in you, he will quiet you with his love, he will rejoice over you with singing." This is the harmony we all seek. It cannot be found in spiritually abusive environments.

Please know that this chapter is not meant as a blanket condemnation of churches and religious organizations. I firmly believe people should be part of a faith community and make it a practice to join with this community regularly in worship and praise to God. God made us to be part of a fellowship of believers, to die to self, and to submit to those placed in authority over us, whether governments or religious leaders. So how can we find our balance? Here are some ways.

- Commit to maintaining a deep, personal relationship with God, in Christ, through the Holy Spirit.
- Do not turn over the responsibility for that relationship to any other person.

- While understanding that leaders are people, hold their actions accountable to Scripture.
- While understanding that leaders are people, hold their words and teachings accountable to Scripture.
- Look for leaders who make themselves accountable to those they lead.
- Look for leaders who have a servant's heart and are humble, contrite, and full of grace.
- Look for churches and organizations whose mission is to help the less fortunate and to strengthen their members for personal godliness.
- Look for churches and organizations whose main concern is to be a part of God's working in the world.
- While understanding that churches and organizations have a need for money, look for one that does not exhibit a love of money.

For those of you who have been emotionally abused, a strong, caring, and compassionate faith community is a place for restoration and healing. It is my fervent prayer that you are a part of such a community and fellowship of believers. If you are not, I urge you to search for one. Many are available, so don't get discouraged and stop searching. There are many wonderful churches and faith communities that do not use fear, guilt, and shame as the battering rams to break down your resistance.

Recognize that a spiritually abusive environment may not appear to be so at first. However, if you are alert to the hallmarks talked about in this chapter, it will become apparent.

If you are involved with a spiritually abusive church or organization, I urge you to find a way to leave it. Your motivation to leave should be so you will be able to better understand and grow in faith yourself. God will not abandon you, no matter what lies you may have been told. Yes, Christ said in Luke 13:24 that the way to heaven is narrow, but it's not so narrow as to encompass only a single church or denomination. God is bigger than that. His love is bigger than that. His grace is bigger than that.

A Time to Heal

God is our heavenly Father and the ultimate authority figure in our lives. Because he is unseen, we often reflect onto him the characteristics and attitudes of our earthly parents and authority figures. Sometimes this reflection is an accurate one because of the exemplary nature and character of those involved. If you have been emotionally abused, the reflection the abusers cast upon your understanding of God is warped and distorted. In order to truly understand God, you need to uncover and reject those distortions.

Take a minute and write down five characteristics of God.

1. _____
2. _____
3. _____
4. _____
5. _____

You might have written something such as the following:

1. God is all-powerful.
2. God judges everyone.
3. God hates and will punish sin.

4. God calls us to be perfect.

5. God sees everything we do.

If you put down a list like this, do you see how it portrays God as a judging, condemning, quick-to-strike, omnipotent being? Ask yourself, is anything on that list untrue? Now, hold that thought as we continue.

You might have written another type of list:

1. God is love.

2. God forgives sin.

3. God is all around.

4. God calls all people to himself as our heavenly Father.

5. God is a gracious God.

This list portrays God as a loving, compassionate, gracious Father. Ask yourself, is anything on that list untrue?

What does your own list tell you about how you view God?

Now think of the person or people who emotionally abused you in the past. What sort of characteristics did they have? Do you see any similarities between your view of God and your view of those people? Do you assume God, as a "superparent" or "super authority" over you, will act the same way, only more so?

After you looked over each list I came up with, I asked if anything on it was untrue. In my understanding, God is all-powerful, he judges everyone, he hates and punishes sin, he calls us to be perfect, and he is able to see everything we do. He is also the embodiment of love, he forgives sin, he is all around, he calls all of us to himself as our heavenly Father, and he is gracious. God is all that and more. When we choose to concentrate on either one list or the other, we fail to see and understand God in the full picture of Scripture, of both the Old Testament and the New Testament.

Which view of God do you normally gravitate toward? Why is it important for you to see God in this way? Who in your past most emulates these attributes of God?

Is it difficult for you to see God in the other view? Why is it so hard? Who in your past most emulates these attributes of God?

God must be allowed to speak for himself. He must be allowed to appear as he is, unclouded by the shadows of people in our past. Especially if you have been emotionally abused, you must allow God to establish his identity free from earthly entanglements in your life. With all my heart, I believe God is able to gently lead you to a fuller understanding of who he is, how much he loves you, and how precious you are to him. This vital spiritual journey is hindered by an abusive spiritual environment. God must be allowed to speak for himself.

Isn't it time to stop relying on what people say about God and start learning for yourself about his love, compassion, majesty, and plan for your life?

If there is one thing holding you back from delving deeper into a personal relationship with God, what is it? Are you willing to let go of it? If so, try praying the following prayer: *Dear Father, I hold this barrier up to you. It is a wall between you and me. Help me to understand that it is a wall of my own making. Help me to understand that you have broken down all the barriers on your side and eagerly wait for me to dismantle this barrier on my side. Give me strength and courage to tear it down. Protect me while I do so. Banish my fear and shame. Quiet my anger and regret. Sing to me and draw me closer to you.*

Part 3

THE EFFECTS
OF EMOTIONAL
ABUSE

In this section we will look more in depth at the many negative effects of emotional abuse. Although they remain interrelated, I have grouped them into three categories to help you process what they have meant in your own life.

Effects on Sense of Self

low self-esteem   acting out sexually
lack of self-confidence   loneliness
transfer of needs   failure syndrome

perfectionism

unrealistic guilt

crisis oriented

unresolved anger and resentments

Physical Effects

addictions

allergies/asthma

depression

anxiety

digestive disturbances

eating disorders

hypochondria

chronic fatigue syndrome

migraine headaches

panic attacks

phobias

unexplained skin rashes

unexplained physical pain

Effects on Relationships

lack of intimate relationships

codependency

inappropriate relationships

isolation from others

excessive compliance or passivity

8

The Effects on Sense of Self

Emotional abuse casts a shadow that hides the light of your
true self.

Andrea couldn't stand to be alone; she just didn't know it. At
home by herself, usually at night, she would panic—heart
racing, hyperventilating, sure she was having a heart attack.
The attacks would come upon her suddenly, in the middle
of watching television or after cleaning up the kitchen. Terrified, she tried to calm herself, but when that proved futile,
the fear would accelerate as she convinced herself something
was physically wrong. After her third visit to the emergency
room in as many weeks, a hospital caseworker suggested that
her health difficulties might better be addressed by a therapist
than a physician. Andrea had never considered counseling
before—it seemed too intrusive and personal—but she was
desperate, unable to hold her debilitating fear at bay.

Even though desperate, Andrea arrived at The Center
guarded, wary, and on edge. She just wanted something,
anything, to stop the panic attacks. She insisted that the only

reason she had come in was because the hospital suggested it. What she wanted was medication. What she got was the truth about herself.

Andrea came to realize that because of emotional abuse she had endured as a child, she never felt truly comfortable with herself. Instead, she derived her sense of self from other people. Andrea strove to please those around her and to do the best job possible. She was a perfectionist when it came to her job. She was at her best in the midst of a busy, bustling office with a high level of demands. When Andrea had something to do, she knew who she was. Growing up, being busy meant being away from home, and that meant she was out of range of an unhappy, bitter mother and a demanding, capricious father. If you weren't busy, you were noticed. If things were quiet, there was no place to hide.

Living in a household where an emotional attack was always a real possibility, Andrea grew up never feeling safe or being totally able to relax. As long as people were surrounding her and things were going on, Andrea was able to divert her growing anxiety and panic into tasks and activity. It was at home, in the quiet, that panic took the upper hand. In order to heal, Andrea needed to learn to relax and be herself—something she had never had the luxury of doing while growing up and something she had never given herself permission to do as an adult. Andrea needed to learn to like who she was, even with nobody else in the room.

Any kind of abuse, emotional abuse included, is an attack on a person's sense of self. It demeans and controls that person through words or actions, devaluing that person and ultimately elevating the abuser. If you have suffered emotional

abuse in your past or are suffering it in the present, it is not something to be ignored, denied, accepted, or perpetuated. The damage it does to your sense of self is pervasive and destructive. Over the course of my years of working with the abused and abusers, I have found several distinct negative effects to the sense of self associated with emotional abuse:

- low self-esteem
- lack of self-confidence
- transfer of needs
- acting out sexually
- loneliness
- failure syndrome
- perfectionism
- unrealistic guilt
- crisis oriented
- unresolved anger and resentments

Depending on your situation, you may find that one or more of these effects is true in your own life. You may have been aware of these effects without understanding why they exist in your life.

Low Self-Esteem

People with high self-esteem are independent thinkers who do not merely accept someone else's word as a basis for their actions but rather evaluate the opinions of others against their own sense of who they are and what they wish to accomplish. It is not that they disregard the thoughts of others, but they do not automatically give those thoughts more value than their own.

Over time the emotional abuser deflates your self-esteem in order to control your thoughts and actions. If you have low self-esteem, you will habitually give in to the desires and demands of others because you distrust your own ability to make competent decisions. A person with high self-esteem, however, is not easily controlled by someone else, especially if that someone wishes to place him or her in an oppressive position. By lowering your self-esteem, the abuser is able to link you to himself or herself by an invisible chain of fear and doubt—fear of the abuser and doubt of your ability to function apart from the abuser.

If you are suffering from low self-esteem, you may have tried unsuccessfully in the past to get beyond it. You may have even found yourself successful to some degree once you were able to remove yourself from the abusive situation. But now, years later, you may find yourself overreacting to an event or comment that consciously or unconsciously reminds you of the past abuse. You may have thought you were successfully over that period in your life only to have it continue to haunt you when you least expect it.[1]

Lack of Self-Confidence

Along with low self-esteem comes a general lack of self-confidence. You may find it difficult to make decisions. After any decision is finally made, you may have second thoughts about it, even change your mind several times. Unable to make decisions on your own, you may seek out others to validate your judgment, even giving in to someone else's persuasive argument although it goes against your gut feeling. Because of this low self-esteem and lack of self-confidence, you may purposely seek out people and work situations that do not threaten your sense of what you are able to accomplish. You may deliberately take jobs that do not stretch your abilities, choosing those you feel you can easily master and never going any farther for fear of failure. Or you may find a way to avoid working with other people altogether, taking a job that infrequently brings you into contact with others. While this provides you with a sense of comfort by controlling what you are able to expect on your job, it can shortchange what you are actually able to accomplish.

Self-confidence allows people to experience risk and bounce back from the setback of failure because they have a basic belief in their own ability to learn and succeed. Low self-confidence avoids risk because of an ingrained belief that risk will always bring failure, a kind of personal Murphy's Law—"Anything I can do wrong, I will do wrong."

Transfer of Needs

All of us have a need to feel special and appreciated, to feel that we have value, to feel good about ourselves. Because of the abuse you have suffered, the fulfillment of this need to feel special and validated by those around you has been absent. To fill that need, you learned as a child to substitute something else for it.

In my work as a counselor, I deal with people who suffer from addictions of all kinds: alcohol dependency, sexual addiction, eating disorders, and drug dependency. As I work with these individuals to help them overcome their addictions, I often find that emotional abuse is the key to their destructive patterns, especially in situations in which physical or sexual abuse is absent. Too often they were the recipients of negative messages that not only robbed them of a positive sense of self but drove them to find solace in inappropriate and destructive sources.

Addictions can be as varied as the people who suffer them. Often workaholics strive to perform out of a sense of necessity, convinced they are worth only what they can accomplish, convinced they have no worth outside of the product of their labors. Instead of alcohol or drugs masking the pain they feel, they have become addicted to work.

Because we all are unique individuals, our responses to filling that unmet need for approval, for validation of our personhood, also will be unique. Take a look at your life and determine those things from which you derive your greatest sense of self-worth. If those sources have nothing to do with who you are but rather what you do, you have transferred your need to feel significant to an inappropriate area.

If you are struggling with an addiction of some kind, you may find it hard to give up because it fills a void in your life, if only for a little while. But the space you are trying to fill is probably the one that says you are special just by being you.

Acting Out Sexually

The ability to provoke a sexual response in another person is a form of control. If you have been emotionally abused, you may feel helpless, overwhelmed, and without control. As such you may be especially vulnerable to experimenting and using your sexuality as a way to control those around you. This may initially take the form of dressing in a provocative manner or engaging in sexual jokes or innuendo. The danger of using your sexuality as a means of control is twofold—it distorts your ability to interact with other people without an added sexual component, and it can lead to sexual encounters for the purpose of testing or exhibiting control.

Your value and worth as an individual are not dependent on how attractive you appear to the opposite sex or how much of a sexual competitor you appear to the same sex. Provoking sexual desire in another person is not a standard by which to measure how effective a person you are in this world. We are more than sexual beings. And to be healthy, we need to relate to other people on more than just a sexual front. Sexuality should not color our every relationship.[2]

Loneliness

If there is a constant I have seen in those suffering from emotional abuse, it is loneliness. You may be involved in a relationship with another person, even a good relationship by most standards, but without a healthy relationship with yourself, no matter how many people you know, you will be lonely. Loneliness is not the same as being alone.

At some point during each day, each of us is alone. No one else is around. There's no music playing, no television blaring, no background noise from others. How we feel in that moment of realization determines whether we are merely alone or also lonely.

Loneliness is not dependent, however, just on our being alone. It can come upon us in the midst of a crowd of people or at the center of a fast-paced office or busy household. Loneliness is lack of true connection. As I said earlier, emotional abuse hinders your ability to establish meaningful connections with other people and, more importantly, with yourself.

Failure Syndrome

During the 1984 presidential election, a little-known politician from Colorado soon emerged as the shining hope for the Democratic party. He was ruggedly good-looking, spoke with sincerity and intelligence, and seemed to articulate the environmental awareness many felt was needed in American politics. His name was Gary Hart.

But a funny thing happened on the way to the election. Stories began to surface about Hart's marital infidelities. Slowly they began to erode his support as people questioned his moral character. His wife staunchly stood by his side and denied the stories. Hart even challenged reporters to catch him in the act—and they did. Reporters photographed a young woman entering and leaving Hart's town house late at night.

Hart's ratings began to plummet as people shook their heads in wonder. Why would Hart flaunt his indiscretions in front of the public and press? Especially at so critical a time as a national election? One explanation surfaced that was intriguingly different from the rest: Gary Hart was suffering from failure syndrome. Deep down he didn't feel he was good enough to win, so he subconsciously sabotaged his own campaign by engaging in conduct he knew would cost him the election. It seemed as if he wanted to throw away whatever chances he had at succeeding in a given task.

In my work I have found that many people we would

consider successful feel deep down as if they have cheated somehow to get where they are. Feeling they don't deserve their success, they live with a constant fear that any day they are going to be exposed for what they really are—frauds, totally inadequate for their jobs. They fear their success was simply a fluke and that eventually the truth will catch up to them and they will ultimately fail in humiliation.

The tragedy is that these are truly capable, often highly creative people who distrust their own success. And the reason they distrust their success is because someone convinced them, most likely in childhood, that they weren't worth anything and were destined for failure.

Even though you have worked hard to get where you are today, do you still worry that it will all be taken away from you? Do you worry deep down inside that you will be asked to handle a job that is so far beyond your abilities that everyone will finally see how you have been fooling them all these years? Has the act of failure become easier to bear than the constant strain of impending doom?

If you find yourself doing or saying things that you know will jeopardize your job situation or your relationships and then find yourself at a loss to explain why you would act in such a way, you may be operating under failure syndrome.

Perfectionism

One of the survival mechanisms a child develops to endure emotional abuse is the obsessive preoccupation with doing everything right. Since any slight or even imagined mistake on the child's part results in a negative response, the child spends a great deal of time and energy avoiding doing anything wrong that might attract the attention of the abuser.

The tendency toward perfectionism most often manifests itself in adulthood. This perfectionism in adults may be directed only inward, or it may be transferred outward to those around you, causing you to maintain the same expectations of perfection from others that you have for yourself.

Perfectionism can operate in two ways—both extremely destructive. You may find yourself going to any lengths to excel in whatever you do, taking up great amounts of time and energy, shortchanging your own health and peace of mind in pursuit of the perfect. You may become so focused on your performance that you completely lose sight of those around you, including co-workers and family. Driven to succeed in order to validate your own sense of self-worth, you may force all others away from you. The danger in this approach is that you are actually accomplishing a great deal, and others, removed from the adverse effects of your obsession, may praise you for how much you are able to do, reinforcing your obsessive perfectionism.

On the opposite end of this frenetic activity, your perfectionism may lead you into a state of paralysis. Since every action carries the risk of failure, actions are to be avoided. You may start projects only to leave them lying around for weeks unfinished. As long as the project is unfinished, you haven't actually failed. You can still visualize all of the rewards of success without suffering any of the negative consequences of failure. Your life becomes a series of projects that you have never started or that you have started but never completed.

Unrealistic Guilt

Unrealistic guilt is the effect of emotional abuse that constantly causes you to say, "It's all my fault," and you do mean *all*. So ingrained is the belief that you are to blame for the world's problems that you carry around an oppressive load of guilt about real and imagined shortcomings.

Negative messages were relayed to you from your abuser, who squarely blamed you for whatever problem he or she seemed to be having. If she had trouble sleeping, it was because you were keeping her awake. If he failed at a sales presentation, it was because your lousy mood destroyed his concentration. If she couldn't find whatever she was looking for, it was because you hid it.

You heard over and over again how your actions soured the life of your abuser, so you came to feel guilty for every bad thing that happened to those around you. If your son had a flat tire on his way to work, it happened because you didn't check the tread life on his tires. If your daughter broke up with her boyfriend, it was because you didn't give her just the right advice she needed. If your spouse got a traffic ticket, it was because you sent him or her out to the store to run a quick errand.

With this guilt comes the fear that you will keep doing things to hurt those you really love. You constantly apologize for wrongs and don't really believe it when the response is, "Don't worry. It's not your fault." Deep down you are convinced that it *is* your fault. Things would have turned out so differently if only you had done something else.

Crisis Oriented

Often emotional abuse takes the form of placing the abused in the position of having to save the abuser. After all, your abuser has made you feel that whatever is wrong is your fault. If it's your fault, it must be your responsibility to fix it. You then desperately try to win back your abuser's favor by fixing whatever problem the abuser seems to be having. The child who is emotionally neglected by his mother may find the only way to be with her is when he is acting as her buddy or confidant. The person whose father is an abusive alcoholic may hear words of thanks or apology only when she is carrying him to his bed or cleaning up his vomit.

As an adult, the abused person becomes crisis oriented, thriving on being the one who fixes everything. If crises don't happen regularly enough to satisfy the need to rush in and act as the knight in shining armor, the abused person may create crises or blow up normal, everyday events or problems into crises of immense proportions.

If you are crisis oriented, you may find that crises provide you with a sense of significance. For a while, it may even bring you accolades, positive attention, and gratitude. But people can only handle so many crises before they get tired of them and of you manufacturing them. They may become so hardened to your manufactured crises that they fail to appreciate any real ones.

Crisis-oriented people feel in control when they are managing a crisis. Because of their dysfunctional past, they may have had a life of crises growing up. They have learned improperly that crises are normal, crises are manageable, crises are energizing, and therefore crises are necessary.

Unresolved Anger and Resentments

Underlying so many effects of emotional abuse is unresolved anger that stems from:

> the seething, violent sense that you have been treated unfairly
>
> the sure knowledge that no matter how hard you tried, it never made any difference
>
> the terrible fear that it was really all your fault they treated you that way
>
> the debilitating realization that you were an idiot to think and hope that someday they would change

Because the emotional abuse has been overlooked and ignored for so long, it has been difficult to give a reason for all of your anger. This anger has been left unresolved because its source has gone unrecognized.

Unresolved anger has a way of venting, even if it spews in inappropriate directions. One of the telltale signs of emotional abuse I look for is if the person has a tendency to suddenly erupt in anger at inconsequential events. As one adage goes, "An *odd* reaction is an *old* reaction." And the saying "The straw that broke the camel's back" presupposes there was an awful lot of straw loaded on that camel's back before the last piece finally broke it.

If you have been emotionally abused in the past, you could be carrying around a load of straw of which you aren't even aware. The tendency to erupt in anger is a signpost of a deeply sensitive, hurting place in your life—an emotional bruise that causes you to wince every time it is touched.

All of these effects of emotional abuse have come about through the verbal and nonverbal messages you received from those who were abusing you. These messages caused you to doubt yourself, sabotaging your sense of self. They made you afraid of your own shadow and suspicious of the people around you. They have subtly influenced your ability to have a positive relationship with yourself. They also have affected your ability to establish and maintain positive relationships with others.

A Time to Heal

The effects of emotional abuse on your sense of self are significant. Yet often these effects are not linked to the emotional abuse you have suffered. Because this connection has not been made, you may find yourself suffering from one or several of these effects without really understanding why.

Here again is the list of effects of emotional abuse:

- low self-esteem
- lack of self-confidence
- transfer of needs
- acting out sexually
- loneliness
- failure syndrome
- perfectionism
- unrealistic guilt
- crisis oriented
- unresolved anger and resentments

1. Go over these effects and honestly evaluate if and how they are present in your own life.

2. Which ones are the most debilitating to you today?

3. As you look at these, are there some you've been able to overcome? How?

4. God is not happy with the list above. He never intended that list to overshadow your life. Instead, he has another list he wants for you. It is found in Galatians 5:22–23:

   - love
   - joy
   - peace
   - patience
   - kindness
   - goodness
   - faithfulness
   - gentleness
   - self-control

   Explain how your life will be different with God's list guiding your life and thoughts.

5. Using God's list, write down at least one way to counter each of the effects of emotional abuse.

6. In question 2, you listed the destructive patterns that are most debilitating in your life today. Which characteristic from God's list do you want to substitute for one of those? Why?

7. Realistically, what will it take for you to begin to substitute the characteristics from God's list for the negative consequences of your emotional abuse? What is the first step you need to take?

8. Look again over the list of negative effects. Is there one or more negative patterns you fear you won't be able to overcome? If so, why?

9. Is there one or more negative patterns you are not ready to give up? If so, why?

10. Write out the following: *Through his Spirit, God has promised me a life full of love, joy, peace, patience, kindness, goodness, faithfulness, gentleness, and self-control. Today I claim this promise from God. I believe in the ability of his Spirit to transform my life.*

Countering the lies of emotional abuse with the truth about our true nature and value as individuals is important. For help in doing that, read over the following statements of commitment. Meditate on them and visualize the positive difference living out these commitments will make in your life.

My Commitment to Myself

1. To believe in my true value.
2. To reject the lies of emotional victimization.
3. To pray that God's love would increase in my life.
4. To learn more about my true self, not my abused self.

One of the most important commitments you can make to yourself is to substitute the negative effects of emotional abuse with positive, affirming characteristics. I cannot think of a better list to strive for than the fruit of the Spirit talked about in Galatians 5:22–23. May these be yours more and more each day.

9

The Physical Effects

The cumulative effect of emotional abuse on an individual often surfaces through physical symptoms.

Catherine was having an affair. It was her little secret. No one else was let in on it, not even her best friend. Her husband didn't know, of course. Every time she would meet with her lover in a quiet room in an out-of-the-way place where no one knew her, she knew it was wrong. But her lover met needs she had in a way nothing else seemed to. Even though she would feel dirty afterwards, it didn't stop her from going, and she would devise elaborate lies to cover up what she was doing.

Even when they were apart, Catherine's mind was on her beloved: when they would meet, what they would do together, how it would feel when it was just the two of them alone again. As she thought of their time together, she could almost begin to hate what they did enough to stop it. But life without her lover seemed like no life at all.

It might have been different if Catherine's lover had been another person, but Catherine was a bulimic, and her lover was food—preferably sweets, chocolate in particular. She would find a safe place, away from prying eyes, and consume mass quantities of cakes, cookies, doughnuts, and desserts of any kind. Shoving them down her throat as fast as she could, she felt as if her hunger was just on the verge of being satisfied. It was always on the verge, though. So she would stuff more and more down in the hope of achieving fulfillment.

Afterwards she would panic. Finding a bathroom, she would turn on the water full blast to hide the noise and stick her finger down her throat.

Something inside Catherine's mind drove her to act out this destructive scenario over and over with her body. Not content to keep the abusive effects to itself, the mind was determined to take the body along with it.

Earlier I talked about how fear, guilt, and anger combine in emotional abuse to damage a person (see chapter 3). Up until now the damage described has been primarily emotional or mental. But it is important to remember that our minds and bodies are linked. What we feel emotionally, we experience physically.

All of us have felt heart-pounding horror at some event, like walking down a dark, deserted street and suddenly hearing footsteps behind us. Our heart races, our respiration quickens, our muscles tense. Adrenaline flows into our system, supercharging us for action. We experience the fight-or-flight response to stimulus.

When this response becomes less an occasional occurrence and more a way of life, there are bound to be physical effects on the body. In my work with a variety of disorders, I have found that each of these different emotions—fear, anger, and guilt—is felt in specific areas of the body, as if each emotion takes up residence in a particular room.

Fear is most often experienced in the stomach. This can be referred to as a gut reaction. Anger appears to be located in the head. The face turns red, blood vessels become distended and pop out, sweat pores enlarge, and breathing increases. Guilt seems to produce an overall bodily reaction.

Through my work I have been able to identify certain physical conditions that indicate to me the presence of emotional abuse as well as other types of abuse:

addictions	chronic fatigue syndrome
allergies/asthma	migraine headaches
depression	panic attacks
anxiety	phobias
digestive disturbances	unexplained skin rashes
eating disorders	unexplained physical pain
hypochondria	

Fear, guilt, and anger produce anxiety, frustration, and hopelessness. When these emotions and feelings are constantly present, the body reacts by producing chemicals designed to stimulate the body to either fight or flee. Because often neither of these responses is appropriate to the situation, the body has to deal with the chemical aftermath these emotions can produce.

Addictions

Emotional abuse leaves deep hurting places in the inner being of the abused. Your abuse may have left you feeling fearful, guilty, and angry over what happened to you. These are unpleasant emotions at best and destructive, harmful emotions at worst. One way many have found to combat the harmful effects of these emotions is to cover them with a physical addiction to any of a variety of substances.

Alcoholism and drug use can provide what seems to be a way of numbing the pain you feel. Pain fades and memory fades when under the influence of the drug of your choice. The relief from pain produces pleasure, but there's always a morning after for the night before. Whatever numbing or pleasurable feeling is achieved is only temporary. So the behavior must be repeated over and over to provide even temporary relief. With many addictive substances, the body begins to tolerate the drug, forcing a higher dosage to be used each time to achieve the same effect, thus feeding the addiction further.

In addition to alcohol and drugs, people can also become addicted to food, sex, and work—anything that allows them to travel outside of themselves for a while, to forget who they really are and how they feel.

The compounding problem of so many physical addictions is that they begin as a direct response of the mind to combat an emotional trauma and end up involving the body as well. Now not only do you have the emotional abuse to work through, you also have the physical addiction to recover from.

Negative Emotionality

Negative emotionality is an ingrained negative response to life and its situations. Emotional abuse and its effects can cause you to develop a view of the world and a response to life that is essentially negative. You simply become trained to think pessimistically. You react negatively to life and you feel bad. This can be partnered with emotional abuse in the worst way—you are convinced the worst will happen, and the emotional abuse tells you it should. You physically feel bad, and the stress of the emotional abuse and its effects contribute to a lack of vitality and health. A National Institute of Alcohol Abuse and Alcoholism study found a link between adolescent alcohol use and negative emotionality.[1] It indicated that further study was needed to determine why. I would venture to say that at the root of much adolescent negative emotionality is a pattern of childhood emotional abuse that is predisposing these young people to feel lousy—physically and about life in general. In an attempt to self-medicate their pain, they use the most readily available drug possible—alcohol.

Allergies/Asthma

Recent evidence has shown that many allergies, especially to molds, can be triggered by stress. Allergies are an inappropriate reaction of the body's immune system to foreign matter. In other words, the body incorrectly identifies mold, dust, pollen, or a food substance as a threat to the body and triggers the arsenal of its immune system to combat the enemy. All the body's defenses rush to force the intruder out of the body. The eyes swell with tears, flushing out impurities. The nose begins to run and you sneeze, blowing the nasal passages clear. The throat becomes ticklish and you cough, forcing the lungs clear. The heart begins to beat faster, increasing circulation.

A positive correlation exists between feelings of stress and allergic reactions. It is as if the body is on alert, so sensitive to any change in condition that it begins to attack substances that normally would be considered benign.

Likewise, asthma has been linked to high levels of stress in individuals, especially those dealing with perfectionism. The anger and feelings of resentment present in those who suffer from perfectionism constantly force the body into a state of alert, often triggering an asthmatic attack.

A woman I dealt with came to me on the recommendation of a medical doctor. She was experiencing trouble breathing. It got to the point where she was gasping for breath at the slightest exertion. She felt something was medically wrong, but the doctor had been unable to find an organic cause for the tightness in her chest. He felt there had to be a psychological explanation for her physical problem, so he sent her to me.

As I talked with her, I found out she lived in a very abusive relationship with a husband who beat her and her children. Not only did he beat her physically, he also beat her emotionally. She could do nothing right, say nothing right. Her life from morning to night was filled with fear and anxiety. Subconsciously she focused the stress she was feeling into her throat and lungs.

The doctor who sent her to me said, "I can't find anything to explain this closing of her air passages, but if something doesn't change, she'll suffer respiratory failure within a year."

This woman was trying so hard to keep all of her feelings bottled up inside that she was slowly suffocating herself. Over the course of that year, I was able to help her realize what her mind was doing to her body. Then she was able to express the anger and frustration she was feeling instead of bottling it up inside.

Depression

As you have been reading, the negative effects of emotional abuse can be overwhelming and debilitating. This can lead to a state of depression when the effects of the abuse compromise your ability to hope, to cope, to envision a future, and to find the strength to carry on each day. Without optimism, it is difficult to drown out many of the negative messages you heard growing up that damaged your emerging sense of self. When these negative messages become too loud and strident to overcome, physical depression can be the result.

I have seen over and over that people will come into counseling in an attempt to overcome depression. They are baffled as to why they are feeling depressed and unsure how to get over it. They want answers to "fix" the problem; they want drugs to "fix" the problem. At the heart of so much of the depression I have treated is emotional abuse as children. Because they are now adults, they can't see how what happened to them twenty, thirty, even forty years ago could make such a difference. Often they have spent their entire adult lives "moving on" and attempting to put the past behind them. What I help them learn is that it is only possible to move on from the past once you have acknowledged and dealt with it. I also help them to see that the ways they have chosen to put the past behind them end up pushing the patterns of the past to the forefront. Ignoring the past doesn't make it go away. Accepting the past does.

Depression has been described as a deep, black hole you find yourself falling into. The sides are steep and slick. There doesn't seem to be any way to stop your descent. It happens in slow motion—flailing of the arms, twists and turns of the body, agonizing movements that produce no results. Eventually you stop fighting and just slide down into the pit. No light. No desires. No energy. No hope.

But also no pain. No anger. No emotions to deal with at all. Just a numbing grayness hanging over your life. When pain is too great, anger too consuming, and emotions too conflicting, the blurry haze of depression has an allure.

Emotional abuse leads to intense feelings of anger, rage, resentment, and bitterness. Submerged feelings of guilt and fear of your abuser can lead you to choose a safer target for your anger than your abuser. All too often that target is you. Unspent anger continually works inside the body, using up energy, causing feelings of fatigue and apathy. Unable to see any hope in your life, you slowly begin to isolate yourself from others, from getting out and socializing, from exercising or taking care of your body. So often in your abuse nothing has seemed to work. Every time you thought it was going to get better, it got worse. *So what's the use?* you wonder.

This world we live in can be a difficult place. Pressures and stresses that come from everyday living are enough to temporarily sideline even the healthiest of us. When emotional abuse has battered your defenses, maintaining a successful stand against those forces can be almost impossible. That is why it is so important to gain support and strength from others: from healthy relationships, from friends who love you, even from caring professionals who can assist you in rediscovering your strength to face each day successfully. You may also need a professional to assist you in rebalancing your body's natural chemistry when necessary.[2]

Anxiety

Emotional abuse, along with other forms of abuse, robs you of a sense of security. Under constant emotional and verbal attack, you learn never to let down your guard, never to relax. The toll of constant vigilance can be an anxiety disorder.

You may experience anxiety in specific situations or a sort of free-floating anxiety that is just waiting for an unguarded moment to pounce. At the root is a deep-seated fear and surety of disaster. This can be brought about by a pervasive pattern of emotional abuse. If you have experienced a reason to be fearful and have felt the devastation of an emotional attack, you may find yourself predisposed toward unhealthy levels of anxiety.

I have people come to me complaining of a general sense of unease, of impending doom, but without a real cause behind it. Unsure about their ability to make decisions, they feel as if something bad is about to happen to them. They most often are highly pessimistic in nature and bitter about what life has dealt them. Sure of disaster around the next corner, they generally have a way of finding it.

Living with emotional abuse sets up a pattern in which nothing is safe, no moment is left unguarded. Everyone must be watched. All precautions must be taken. Every contingency must be planned for. This makes for an individual who is always on guard.

Often such people are called high-strung or nervous. What they are experiencing is a continual state of anxiety. If the abused is no longer in an abusive situation, the reason for the anxiety no longer exists, but the pattern remains. Without a focus, it remains free-floating—a constant sense of apprehension without a concrete source.

Fear of abuse has become a permanent feature etched on the inner being of the abused. If fear was the one strong emotion you grew up with, if fear proved useful to you in the past by alerting you to danger, then fear becomes a normal way of processing information in the present. But fear leads to anxiety.

Digestive Disturbances

Our digestive systems are made up of an enormous network of muscles and chemicals all working in harmony to process the foods we eat. When you find yourself under stress, muscles all over the body begin to contract and knot. Chemical levels in the bloodstream are altered. Is it any wonder, then, that so many people experience stress in their stomachs? Heartburn, acid indigestion, gas, ulcers, diarrhea, and constipation can all be physical signs of emotional stress.

Of course, these symptoms can have very real physical causes, but in our hectic, fast-paced lives, we often don't eat what we should. We also don't take time to relax when we eat. This stress on our bodies can produce digestive problems. Compounding that are the food allergies we can develop because of our eating patterns. Too much fat and sugar and too many wheat products, which are so plentiful in modern processed food, can trigger an overload in our systems, producing an allergic reaction to those and other substances.

A person who has been emotionally abused isn't used to being completely relaxed. The abused must be always on the lookout for the abuser. Fear of the abuser haunts every moment. Muscles rarely relax; underlying or overt muscular tension is always present. Digestive juices continue to churn, even if there is no food to digest. Eventually this leads the stomach to, in essence, digest itself. When it does so, holes in the stomach lining result, producing ulcers.

Eating Disorders

Bulimia, anorexia, and compulsive overeating all have their roots in abuse of some kind. They derive from an inappropriate use of control. The bulimic and the compulsive overeater are out of control. The compulsive overeater is a binge eater, like the bulimic, without the subsequent purging. For the anorexic, the problem isn't a lack of control, it is the obsessive use of control—specifically control over one's consumption of food.

No one starts out life deciding they are going to spend years stuffing sweets and junk food down their throats only to throw it up or flush it out of the body with laxatives and diuretics. No one starts out life deciding they are going to drink only water and take four bites of food each day to force their body to shrink. No one starts out that way.

Rarely have I found elsewhere the intensity of anger that I find in anorexics. After a period of slow starvation, it seems as if anger is the only thing fueling their shrunken bodies. Their eyes burn with anger and their jaws remain clenched with it. The rigid control they exert over their own ability to feel hunger is their compulsive attempt to control their anger. Control their hunger—control their bodies—control their anger.

Somewhere along the line, messages were given to all these individuals about their self-worth, their looks, their weight, and their value to themselves and others. Those messages, delivered under the battering of emotional abuse, gave birth to the destructive practices of the eating disorder.[3]

Hypochondria

For some people, anxiety can eventually lodge in their bodies, causing a variety of physical discomforts. Often they experience chronic symptoms that elude medical diagnosis. It is obvious to them that they have a problem, but their doctor is unable to find it. Too often in the past, mood-altering drugs have been prescribed to calm such a case of nervousness.

With hypochondria, a multitude of physical complaints, usually minor and non–life-threatening, plague a person. Sometimes hypochondria can manifest itself in a disease-of-the-month syndrome. You read of someone who experienced a particular disease, a certain symptom, and sure enough, you find you have it too. Such preoccupation with your own body and physical health leads to a hyperfocus on every ache and pain, pimple and twinge you may have. It provides an outlet for free-floating fear and anxiety.

Chronic Fatigue Syndrome

Sometimes the body becomes so worn down it compromises its ability to repair and rejuvenate. When this happens, a person can feel exhausted and run-down all the time. For years this condition existed without a name. It is now known as chronic fatigue syndrome. I strongly suspect that some of those who suffer from chronic fatigue syndrome are feeling its debilitating effects because of the stress of unacknowledged emotional abuse in their past or present relationships.

Emotional abuse produces negative feelings and emotions that constantly assault the body and its systems. Over time this wears down the body and can compromise its maintenance and repair processes. Unable to fully rejuvenate and repair itself, illness can occur, further impairing the body's ability to achieve healing. The body is stressed, tired, and weak from fighting off illness after illness. It may reach a point, such as in chronic fatigue syndrome, at which proactive, aggressive measures need to be taken to boost recovery.

Migraine Headaches

Blood is pounding in your head. Your temples feel like they are about to explode. Any amount of light sends piercing stabs of pain through your eyes. Movement is nauseating, sound unbearable. The only way to cope is to lie perfectly still. No light. No sound. No movement. Only a slow countdown until the pain diminishes enough for you to realize you are going to live, or even want to live.

One of the most debilitating responses of the body to stress is a migraine headache. Silent stalkers, they attack unannounced, rendering you incapable of tolerating stimuli of any kind. There is no way to work around this effect. It knocks you flat on your back and keeps you there.

Researchers are still studying why stress triggers this reaction, but it has been associated with low self-esteem, extreme perfectionism, and the accompanying feelings of anger, fear, and guilt. Much more work needs to be done to understand and treat these intense and painful episodes.

Low self-esteem and perfectionism are two characteristics of people who have undergone prolonged emotional abuse in their past. In my work I have found that migraine headaches are, unfortunately, another characteristic.

Panic Attacks

It all started with an elevator. Janice was taking the elevator up to her usual floor at work one day when the elevator malfunctioned. She was trapped inside for hours until someone was finally able to get it working properly again.

As hard as that was to overcome, Janice was beginning to put it behind her and get a proper perspective on the traumatic event when lightning struck a second time. Janice loved to take out-of-town friends to the Space Needle restaurant in downtown Seattle. Towering high over the city, the restaurant affords a revolving view of the skyline as patrons dine.

To get to the restaurant circling atop the Space Needle, diners ride in an elevator that has windows along its side providing a view of the surrounding area. On Janice's way up, the elevator broke. Twice in as many months Janice had to endure the trauma of being trapped in a nonfunctioning elevator. This time the elevator had windows, so she could see just how dangerous a position she was in.

For a while afterward Janice was able to go on with her life. But soon the thought of even stepping into an elevator was nauseating, so she took the stairs. But then even the thought of being up that high, no matter how she got there, caused intense panic attacks. Her heart would race, she would become dizzy and light-headed, and she would hyperventilate. Eventually she was forced to give up her job because she was no longer physically able to make it to the twelfth floor.

When Janice finally came to see me, she couldn't even travel up a flight of stairs without having a panic attack. The attacks were so strong she was sure she was going to die of a heart attack. She had a two-story house, but she started sleeping on the sofa downstairs to avoid climbing above ground level.

Janice had always been a high-strung person. When she was a child, her father was commanding and her mother was demanding. She had grown up very performance driven. Everything needed to be done just so with Janice. Her looks, her dress, her manners, and her work were carried out with precision and control—until she lost control twice in the elevators.

Panic attacks are specific physical events with an emotional or psychological basis. They produce dramatic physical symptoms and can be overwhelming for the person experiencing them. At the root of a panic attack is an abnormally strong fear reaction and the presence of a high level of adrenaline produced by the body in reaction to the fear. This is emotional anxiety given a physical outlet. Emotional abuse intersects with panic attacks when the fear producing the attack comes from an abusive pattern in the past. Janice had always been terrified of losing control because of the emotional abuse suffered as a child. It wasn't until she experienced a physical event—the breakdown of the elevators—that her ever-present subconscious fear found a conscious outlet.

While panic attacks can be intensive and devastating initially, they are also highly treatable. Once Janice learned the true source of her fear, she was able to develop a strategy for confronting it. She no longer fears riding in elevators and has come to closure on much of the emotional abuse in her past.

Phobias

Anxiety can manifest itself in different ways, being tied to different events and running the gamut from acrophobia (fear of heights) to claustrophobia (fear of enclosed spaces) to agoraphobia (fear of open spaces). Often these phobias are as unique as the individual, with common fears including those mentioned along with arachnophobia (fear of spiders) and pyrophobia (fear of fire).

Most of the time these disorders can be treated by going back and discovering the root event that triggered the panic response and then putting it into perspective. Slowly, with support, you can overcome your fears a step at a time. In the case of emotional abuse and phobias, there generally is a specific event or chain of events that has tied the phobia with the abuse. By disconnecting the phobia from the abuse, the strength of the phobia is diminished and the person is better able to work past the fear.

Unexplained Skin Rashes

Have you or anyone you know broken out in hives before an important event? Or did your skin break out in pimples or acne the day before the senior prom? Or have you developed a rash all over your face before a sales presentation?

The skin is a canvas on which our inner emotional state is often painted. Healthy, glowing skin can be a sign of a contented, at-peace individual. Erupting, pimply skin may be a sign of inner turmoil, as any teenager would attest. This is not always the case, though, and there are certainly physical reasons for the skin to break out without emotional issues playing a part. In my work, however, I have found that as individuals are undergoing counseling, they may develop skin problems at particularly stressful times in their recovery.

Unexplained Physical Pain

In his book *Mind over Back Pain*,[4] Dr. John E. Sarno points to an emotional cause for physical pain. In other words, some pain you are experiencing could be your body's way of alerting you to subconscious emotional pain. When a distinct physical cause of pain cannot be found, Dr. Sarno's approach is to look for a psychosomatic cause. The pain is no less real for having a psychological origin.

In my practice I certainly agree with Dr. Sarno. Most often the pain complained of is lower back pain. It seems to be a part of the body where tension, from a variety of sources, is funneled. It is amazing how releasing emotional pain can alleviate physical symptoms of pain.

I remember one woman, Alice, who came to The Center when her physician refused to continue to prescribe pain medication because she was developing an addiction to it.

Alice complained of lower back pain even though X-rays and medical tests could point to nothing physically wrong. The pain was so intense she could rarely sit still during an entire session. Instead, she would need to get up and move around to mitigate the pain, which was written all over her face.

Alice had married young and had given birth to three children in quick succession soon afterward. When her husband left her for another woman, Alice found herself in the position of raising the children on her own without support from him. Now, twenty-five years later, the children were grown, and what she had experienced during her seven-year marriage was the farthest thing from Alice's mind to explain her back pain. As we began to investigate some of the traumatic events of her past, she began to talk about what life was like during her first marriage. The more she talked about it, the more she needed to get up, and the greater the pain became. When I mentioned the connection, Alice didn't dismiss it. Instead, she became very quiet.

Over the course of the next several months, as we worked on the abusive first marriage, Alice was able to significantly reduce the amount of her pain medication. She was able to stay seated longer and even enjoyed the benefits of our massage practitioner. Without realizing it, Alice had learned during those traumatic years to concentrate her stress in one area of her back. She used to sit a certain way on the couch, looking out the window while waiting for her husband to come home. The later he was, the more tense she became. Even after he left, the pain remained, both emotionally and physically. As Alice learned to release the pain, she felt better about herself and about life, and her physical pain greatly decreased.

The effects of emotional abuse rarely remain in the realm of the mental or emotional alone. Invariably, they spread to the other aspects of a person as well. Your physical body is tied to your emotional state. If you are a happy, contented person, your body tends to thrive. If you are an anxious, driven person, your physical body suffers. While you might choose to ignore the signs of emotional abuse in your life, often you have no choice but to pay attention to the physical ones. When the body speaks, it's time to listen. Even if it speaks in a whisper, don't wait until it begins to shout. You may want to consider medical and psychological assistance. By being alert to one part of yourself, your body, and the effects you experience, you can be led to discover the truth about your whole self—emotional, physical, and relational.

A Time to Heal

Few of us truly appreciate just how marvelous our physical bodies are. They are intricate, complex machines, able to withstand a great deal of stress and, frankly, mistreatment. There comes a time, however, when our physical bodies say, "Enough." This is especially true of the stresses produced through constantly undergoing feelings of anger, fear, shame, and guilt, for these emotions exact a physical toll.

Let's look again at the list of physical symptoms from the stress of emotional abuse:

- addictions
- allergies/asthma
- depression
- anxiety
- digestive disturbances
- eating disorders

- hypochondria
- chronic fatigue syndrome
- migraine headaches
- panic attacks
- phobias
- unexplained skin rashes
- unexplained physical pain

1. Which of these conditions are you currently experiencing?
2. Which ones have you experienced in the past?
3. Do you have a chronic condition that appears to defy your attempts to get better?
4. Do medical tests come up normal, but this condition persists?
5. Have you ever considered any of the conditions on the list to be tied to your past emotional abuse?
6. After reading this chapter, do you feel this is a possibility? If so, why? If not, why not?
7. Which of these conditions are the most severe in your life right now?
8. What have you done to get help for these conditions? Are the interventions proving successful?
9. Are you willing to work with mental health and healthcare professionals to address these conditions, or do you feel a need to get better by yourself?
10. Have you tried to get better by yourself in the past? If so, was this successful?
11. If you are not willing at this time to work with mental health or medical professionals, can you identify why?

12. If working with your current mental health or health-care professional is not producing positive results, are you willing to seek help elsewhere?

13. Have you been advised to change your habits or behaviors in order to achieve positive change for your health? If so, what have you been advised to do?

14. Have you found that you are able to make those changes? If not, why not?

15. Are you willing to change your lifestyle and food intake to help achieve health and recovery?

Though the body's systems are remarkably complex, the components necessary to help the body rebuild itself physically are not. Over the course of my years at The Center helping clients, I have found that there are six commonsense steps anyone can take toward better health. They are:

- *Healthy eating.* What you eat determines how you feel, so choose your food wisely.

- *Nutritional supplements.* A good multivitamin every day is now recommended.

- *Proper hydration.* Water is your body's lubricant—you need more than you think.

- *Curative sleep.* Our hectic lives can rob us of this needed element, so guard your sleep.

- *Physical movement.* Our bodies are made to move, so it's a good idea to exercise every day.

- *Fun and uplifting activities.* Laughter and joy have positive physical effects, so enjoy life!

Our bodies are God's gift to us to enjoy and use to accomplish his purpose for our lives. Taking care of yourself isn't a luxury. It isn't indulgent or selfish. It's necessary. And you are worth living a life of good health and joy.

1. As you look at the six steps you can take, which do you consider most needed in your life today?

2. What would hinder you from adopting that positive step?

3. What would motivate you to take and keep taking that positive step?

4. Can you identify anyone in your life who can act as an encourager or a motivator for you in taking that step? Is there anything hindering you from asking that person?

5. Psalm 38 is an anguished cry from David to the Lord in which David speaks eloquently of the physical manifestation of sin in his life. David's pain and suffering sprang from his own sin, but similar pain and suffering can spring from others' sins against a person. Read over Psalm 38 and see if you have felt the same types of symptoms. What specifically can you identify?

6. David was able to overcome these devastating physical effects because of his understanding of and belief in the love of God. The effects were a reality in David's life for a short time but not the ongoing backdrop of his life. What physical effects are you ready to get help for?

7. What stands in your way of dealing with the other physical effects? What will it take for you to be ready to tackle those?

At The Center, we address the whole person in recovery, combining emotional, relational, physical, and spiritual care. In the same manner, it is important for you to have a whole-person team of professionals working together to address your chronic health concerns.

10

The Effects on Relationships

> If your most fundamental relationships include emotional abuse, that abuse will hinder your attempts to build healthy, positive relationships with yourself, with others, and with God. It is possible, though, to rebuild intimacy in your key relationships through understanding and accepting your true self.

Emotional abuse starts within the framework of a relationship with a parent, sibling, friend, teacher, or employer. The relationships we form with others are meant to give us support, establish a sense of belonging and unity, and fill our emotional and physical needs for comfort and companionship. When abuse is present in our relationships, these needs are not being met and physical or emotional damage is being done.

If you have been involved in an abusive relationship, you may have an inaccurate perception of what makes a good relationship. And because we often tend to go toward the familiar, it should not be surprising that an abusive past relationship can set you up for an abusive present or future relationship.

When emotional abuse damages one relationship, it can affect all the relationships you form with family, friends, and co-workers. Most important, it can damage the relationship you have with yourself. And it can also have a detrimental effect on your spiritual relationship with God.

The Relationship with Self

The world is quiet. No sound from the television to mask inner thoughts. No music from the radio to drown out the cries of the past. No light to distract the inner eye from seeing the way things really are. No presence of other people to overshadow the knowledge of self. Just the late-night/early-morning moment of truth when the only person left to hide from is looking back at you in the mirror.

In chapter 8, I discussed in depth the negative effects emotional abuse can have on your sense of self. How you feel about yourself is the backbone of your relationship with self. If you feel good about who you are as an individual, your relationship with self is supportive and based on realistic expectations. If you have believed the false messages fed to you through abusive people, your relationship with self is fraught with self-doubt, guilt, and frustration.

You can never run away from yourself. You can try, but you will always catch up with yourself in those quiet moments just before dawn when the world is silent and there is no place left to hide. Every time you look in a mirror, you are forced to see who you are. And just as there are mirrors for your eyes, there are mirrors for your soul—those times and events when you truly see who you are.

One of the most damaging things about emotional abuse is that it distorts your vision, causing you to see a false reflection in the mirror. It causes you to distrust what your eyes see and your heart feels deep down. In the darkest moments, when you have isolated yourself from everyone else around you, how you feel about yourself still remains. The relationship with self affects all other relationships you have.

Your Relationship with Your Spouse

Too often the sad truth is that the emotional abuse you have been subjected to was from a member of your own family. Gone was the ideal family with a loving set of parents and close-knit siblings. Instead, something else—something far less ideal—was substituted.

You may have thought that when you grew up, you were over it, that you had escaped from your situation and left it behind you. Often this is not the case, for there are very specific ways that emotional abuse in the past can affect present or future relationships within your adult family.

One of the manifestations of your abuse may be your desire to find a person just like the one who abused you. While this may not seem to make much sense logically, it certainly holds true emotionally. Relationships can be scary. How the other person will feel and react is an unknown. Often, to cut down on the amount of surprise, people look for personality traits with which they are most familiar. If the person who emotionally abused you was a parent of the opposite sex, the chances are you will be drawn to a mate who portrays similar characteristics. If you had a controlling father, you may seek out a man who is opinionated and overbearing. If you had a loud, outspoken mother, you may look for a woman who exhibits the same characteristics. While it is said that opposites attract, there are complex reasons why one person falls in love with another. Subconsciously you may have chosen a mate who mirrors behavior within your new relationship that you are familiar with from a past one.

Unfortunately, this could mean entering into another abusive relationship, with an abusive spouse taking the place of an abusive parent. The emotional abuse in your past may cause you to make inappropriate choices in relationships in the present or future. This is one part of the repeating cycle of abuse, going from one abusive relationship to another.

On the other hand, you may have been able to avoid this pattern by intentionally choosing someone who was nothing like your past abuser. Making this choice, you may have thought you were off the hook. This is not necessarily the case. Even if your current mate is free from abusive behavior, your abusive past can adversely affect your relationship.

Jack watched his wife move around the room. She was gorgeous—beautifully dressed, slim, and tan. He watched the other men watching her. A few gave her lecherous glances, but most were frankly appreciative of what they saw. Part of him felt a sense of pride that he had such a beautiful wife. He knew there were many in the room who wondered, ever so briefly, what it would be like to be in his shoes.

If they only knew, he thought to himself. It wasn't that he didn't love Pat. He did. And it wasn't that he didn't appreciate her physical beauty, because he did. But none of the others in the room knew what it was like to live with her.

Pat never dropped her guard. Always in control of every situation, she lived her life firmly in command. Her daily schedule was totally regimented. She knew what she was going to do nearly every second of every day.

Pat's appearance was also strictly regulated. She spent hours maintaining her sleek, healthy, immaculate appearance. Every aspect of her wardrobe was chosen with the greatest care—and at no small cost. She would fly into a rage about a hair out of place or a pound gained overnight. If she was happy with her appearance, she could smile. If she wasn't, the most she could muster was a polite, bland expression in public and a tight, closed demeanor in private.

Pat's food intake was maintained with near obsessive diligence. Jack might indulge in a late-night snack or occasional hot fudge sundae, but Pat never did. Meals weren't a relaxing time to mull over the day together. To Pat they were brief skirmishes to be won as quickly as possible. He usually ended up finishing his meal alone while Pat flew around the kitchen removing all traces of the dinner.

Jack couldn't burp, pass gas, pick his teeth, or, God forbid, pick his nose anywhere near Pat. She felt natural bodily functions were crude. There wasn't anything relaxing about being around Pat. She was always in control, always accomplishing something, and she expected him to live his life the same way. There was no end to the disappointment he caused Pat when he didn't. He heard about it constantly.

Jack and Pat's sex life was totally controlled by Pat and whether she was in the mood. Since he would never even think of encouraging her when she wasn't in the mood, she always decided when they would have sex. It was a given that he wanted to—a point she made sure to bring up derisively whenever provoked. So whenever she wanted to have sex, he was expected to comply, which, quite honestly, wasn't enough for him. But he loved Pat and waited patiently for those times when she wanted to love him back.

Others saw the Pat she so meticulously presented. He lived with the parts that were left. So he sat back and watched her move around the room, engaging in as much wishful thinking as any man there.

Intimacy, by its very nature, involves allowing another person to enter into our private world. While often associated with physical closeness, true intimacy encompasses an emotional bonding and deep connection. When a person has been emotionally abused, the ability to establish deep emotional bonds is compromised. Often the source of that emotional abuse has come from a past intimate relationship—a spouse, sibling, or parent. Intimate relationships, therefore, are viewed with suspicion and fear. If a relationship is attempted, the abused person may not allow it to reach beyond a surface level, in order to avoid the potential for being hurt; intimacy is simply not worth the risk.

One of the most common relational effects of emotional abuse I have found is an inability to experience intimacy. At the heart of the ability to maintain intimacy is trust. An intimate relationship is one that leaves little room to hide. You open yourself up as completely as you can to another person. The more open you are, the more you can join together.

Abuse destroys trust. In the past, trusting an abusive person only led to pain. Trust, therefore, is something to be avoided, to be suspicious of. But trust is an integral component of a healthy marriage. When it is absent, the relationship suffers.

Within a sexual relationship, the need for trust is crucial. When problems are present in a couple's sexual life, problems tend to multiply in other areas as well. The frustrations of being sexually fearful or unfulfilled can spill over into hurt feelings and repressed anger.

Another damaging offshoot of emotional abuse is perfectionism. Wanting to do things well is hardly a character flaw, but perfectionism is the obsessive need to operate at a perfect level at all times. If this level is not achieved, the perfectionist can react with either extreme anger or apathetic indifference. He or she may say either, "I don't care what you do; I'm not leaving until I get this right," or "What difference does it make anyway? I'll never get it right, so why bother trying at all?"

Perfectionists put themselves under tremendous pressure at all times. Things must be done to their rigid standards, or their whole world comes crashing down. Anyone who happens to be near them gets caught in the crash.

Terry was furious. Her new husband, Brent, was nothing but negative about her new job. When she came home excited about her promotion, he brought up every reason he could think of why the job really wasn't all that great. She had expected him to be excited. After all, it meant a considerable increase in her salary. More money for her meant more money for him, so what was the problem anyway? In a fit of anger, she had even accused him of being jealous. Nothing else seemed to make sense.

Terry had fumed out of the apartment, intent on a nice long drive to blow off some steam. How dare he put her down like that! What was his problem anyway? She had expected a happy, supportive reaction from him and had gotten the exact opposite. Why had he reacted in such a negative manner? Had she really misjudged him so completely? And what did that mean for the future—*their* future?

Brent couldn't believe it when Terry charged out the door. Why in the world had he said what he did? Terry had worked hard for that promotion. She deserved it. It meant more financial freedom for the two of them. Why had such an uneasy feeling washed over him when she had delivered the news? It was as if he was afraid of something, but he couldn't figure out what. All he knew was that Terry telling him about the job had made him feel scared—more than scared—unsafe.

Alone in the quiet apartment, Brent began to backtrack in his mind to the root of his uneasy feeling. He closed his eyes and tried to remember when he had felt that way before. At first, nothing came—no sights, no sounds, no memories at all. He felt himself becoming tense again. Letting out a deep breath, he told himself that it was okay. He moved his neck back and forth trying to relax. Still nothing came.

Then he tried another tactic. Holding a conversation with himself, he asked himself, "What's the worst thing that could happen if Terry takes this job?" As soon as he asked it, he had his answer. "She'll leave you," popped into his head so quickly and so clearly he nearly jumped out of his chair.

"You think she won't need you anymore!" he said to himself in amazement.

By the time Terry returned home, her anger spent but her confusion remaining, Brent was able to sit her down and explain where his fear had come from. Brent's parents had divorced when he was twelve. He didn't see much of his dad after that. They had seen each other a few times and talked on the phone, but his dad had seemed to get along just fine without him, his mom, and his sister. When Brent's dad left, Brent wasn't entirely sad to see him go. Brent's dad had always had a sharp tongue. In fact, Brent could probably count on one hand the number of times his dad had said anything nice to him in the twelve years before he left the family. Brent never seemed to be able to live up to his father's expectations. Consequently, his father was convinced that Brent would never amount to much.

About the only thing Brent's dad thought he did right was to marry Terry. He came to the wedding after not seeing or speaking to Brent in years. But he had come, and Brent distinctly remembered him saying, "Never thought you'd ever find anyone as good as Terry. You just make sure you keep her."

Deep down Brent was afraid he wouldn't be able to.

Terry cried when Brent told her what was really going on inside him. She hugged him close and promised never to leave him, ever. The job was important to her, sure, but he was the most important thing in her life and always would be.

"Stop listening to your dad," she said sternly, while holding him close, "and start listening to me!"

Even if you have married a so-called healthy person and avoided the trap of continuing in an abusive relationship, it doesn't necessarily mean that your own past will have no repercussions in your new relationship. Brent and Terry were a couple who came to me for counseling. Brent needed guidance to overcome his feelings of abandonment and low self-esteem. Terry needed help to understand Brent and how his abusive past was affecting their present relationship. Terry was not a victim of emotional abuse in her life, but when she married Brent she became joined emotionally and physically with someone who was.

As I have said, emotional abuse triggers intense feelings of fear, guilt, and anger. Those emotions can be denied and repressed for years. But eventually they have a way of expressing themselves, often in inappropriate and confusing ways, to both the abused person and those in relationship with him or her.

One of the most common responses is hypersensitivity. Because of an abusive past, you may have developed a radar system tuned to picking up any comment or action from those around you that could be interpreted as negative. If you grew up in a negative environment, that is what you have come to expect. You look for the negative and can usually find it.

When you then react to the negative things you perceive in the actions and comments of others, it is often with an increased response. Your anger is all-consuming. You aren't just angry about what was said yesterday; you are angry at all the hurtful things that were said in all the past yesterdays.

Your guilt is overwhelming. What they said about you the other day was so true. It has been true all your life. Why even try to deny it anymore? You're bad. You're nothing. Why even try?

The emotional responses you feel in the present are very real even though they may be based in large part on past events. Those you are in a relationship with may have no frame of reference for your strong reactions. They simply won't understand why what they said or did caused you to react the way you did, and often you won't either. This can add tension and confusion to your relationships.

Relationships on the Job

In chapter 8, I discussed the failure syndrome as it applies to work situations. It can leave you fearful of being discovered as a fraud or cause you to take jobs that are not challenging to you.

In addition, your working relationships can be affected if the personalities of your boss or co-workers closely approximate someone in your past who emotionally abused you. Your boss could be just like your dad. A supervisor could treat you just like your mother did. A co-worker could remind you of the way a sibling used to talk to you.

Cindy was already seeing me for depression when another problem cropped up. Work had been one of the few places Cindy felt good about herself. Her home life might be a disaster, but at work Cindy felt like she knew what she was doing. Lately, however, the thought of going to work sent her into a panic.

As I reviewed Cindy's work situation, she explained that although she was doing the same job, she had a new supervisor. The previous one had been a friendly, laid-back man who enjoyed jokes and gave Cindy a high degree of freedom to do her job without interference. Her new supervisor was completely different. Rarely smiling, he seemed to Cindy to hover over her desk, alert for anything she might be doing wrong. It wasn't just her; he was like that with the other women in her department.

Soon after he had begun supervising her section, an accounting error had been found. Not a major one, but enough to raise eyebrows. Everyone was understandably nervous about tracking the cause of the error. To Cindy's horror, one of her co-workers intimated to the new supervisor that Cindy was responsible. Instead of asking her about it, he immediately assumed she was at fault. Though the error couldn't be traced back to her, he now treated her as if her work product was inferior to the others. Not only was she working under a suspicious boss, but she had found out just what kind of friend she had in her co-worker.

This would have been a difficult situation for anyone. But as we talked about it, Cindy said to me, "You know, I felt just like I did when my dad used to get mad at me. I was always the one to blame. I could never do anything right. And Mom used to let Dad think that I was at fault. She never stood up for me. I was the scapegoat. That's just how I felt at work when that happened. Like I was a kid again. My boss was my dad, and my friend was my mom. There I was again, taking the blame for something I didn't do!"

Cindy was able to confront her friend about how she had acted and to learn to work for her boss without feeling guilty about doing her job. She had to pull herself away from her past patterns and deal with her work situation in the present. It wasn't long before her boss was transferred to another department where he wasn't responsible for the work product of so many employees.

Our family relationships are the foundation for how we interact with people in the future. If the foundation is shaky, it needs to be shored up with healthy models of positive relationships.

No amount of money is worth staying in an abusive work environment. There are laws now to protect workers from what is known as a hostile work environment as it relates to outright harassment. If you find yourself in a hostile work environment with an abusive person, you should consider looking for another job, even if the law isn't on your side. Is it fair that you should have to leave your job? No. But it might be better for you in the long run.

Your Spiritual Relationship

Whatever your religious background, you probably have come into contact with the concept of God being a higher authority. Often the person in your past who abused you was in a position of authority over you—an adult or an older child. Because of that abuse, it is natural to develop a fear of authority in any form, including spiritual authority. A response to this fear of authority can take two paths. One is to completely reject authority of all kinds, especially spiritual. The other is to wholeheartedly embrace an adult equivalent to the oppressive authority you experienced as a child.

If your response has been to reject all authority, you probably have sworn off religion. After all, religious faith recognizes God's authority as higher than your own and involves conforming your life and actions to his will. If you grew up in a rigid, overbearing relationship with someone in authority, conforming yourself to anyone's will again might be extremely difficult. You may not have had any choice about being under the abusive authority you suffered in the past, but you sure have a say now! And there is no way you are going to get involved with any kind of church with all their rules and regulations! Religion is simply not for you.

The other response is to seek within religion the kind of tight, consuming control you experienced as a child. Often this is the reason many people willingly give up their freedom of choice and join cults, even those destructive cults that ultimately have led to the tragic deaths of the followers, such as those at Jonestown and Waco. Cults usually have a charismatic central figure who is alternately regarded by his or her followers as a god and as a father or mother figure. This type of personality attracts those who are seeking the comfort of a controlling personality who will tell them what to do and give their lives meaning.

Whether the response is to reject all religious authority or seek a controlling cult group, the ability to have a healthy spiritual relationship is hindered because of emotional abuse. Our relationships should support us and give us a sense of belonging and unity. Spiritual relationships can do that in a way that few other relationships can, but only if they are healthy. Spiritual relationships that merely repeat the patterns of past abuse are not fulfilling their proper function. If you have been frustrated in developing your own spiritual relationship, look to your past relationships for evidence of abuse. Find someone to help you stop repeating the same unhealthy patterns in the one relationship you need most.

Your Relationship with Your Children

I have saved this relationship for last because it can be the most difficult to deal with—not because children are the most difficult to deal with, but because if you are a parent, so much of your very self can be tied up in your children.

"Mommy, I hurt myself!" Jessica's youngest ran up to her, tears streaming. Dropping everything, Jessica scooped him up in her arms and comforted him. Two seconds before, he had been trying to get her attention, but she was putting away groceries and had been busy. But now he was hurt, and all her attention was focused on him.

Jessica grew up in an unaffectionate household. No one had ever been there to hold her when she fell or scraped a knee. Now when one of her kids was hurt, she made sure they were treated better than she had been.

What started out as wonderful when they were little soon turned into a problem as they got older. Whenever any of them wanted attention, he or she simply "got hurt." If Mommy was too busy, was too preoccupied with one of the other children or with Daddy, or was talking on the phone, a finger or toe would get hurt, a knee would get bumped, or one of a hundred other small complaints would be loudly proclaimed to ensure that Mommy stopped whatever she was doing and listened.

Eventually it was all Jessica could do to work on one thing for any length of time without being interrupted. Frustrated at all the crying and complaints, she began to respond in anger.

"Why can't you kids leave me alone for just five minutes! I can never get anything done around here without one of you coming up and whining about something!" She would rant and rave for a second or two, but the kids knew nothing would ever come of it. Jessica had trouble disciplining her children. Every time she thought of it, she would remember what it was like growing up. Though she knew her children needed her to set limits on their behavior, she couldn't seem to get past her negative reaction to those limits. As a consequence, Jessica found herself losing control of her children, and instead, they began to control her. When they did, she generally lost control of her anger. It was a vicious cycle that needed to be stopped.

Unfortunately, abuse of all kinds is a vicious cycle that keeps going round and round, from generation to generation. Part of the cyclical nature of abuse is to enter into abusive relationships in the future because of past ones. Within those abusive relationships it is possible for the abused to become the abuser, repeating the pattern of abuse learned at the hands of his or her abuser.

Much research points to the fact that abusers in our society today were themselves abused as children. Many of you who were emotionally abused in the past may find yourselves acting out the abuse you suffered on those around you. Children have always been a convenient target for that abuse.

Emotional abuse can have a devastating effect on all personal relationships. That is why it is so vital if you have been emotionally abused that you acknowledge the fact of that abuse, no matter how painful the realization, and actively learn how to overcome its effects.

Codependency

Relationships between people are healthy when they are interconnected. In an interconnected relationship, each person has his or her own needs met and strives to meet the needs of the other person. A problem occurs, however, when relationships are not just interconnected but are codependent. In codependent relationships, the needs of one person being filled by the other are unhealthy or inappropriate. One of the most common scenarios of codependency is an alcoholic who is routinely supplied with liquor by the other person in the relationship, even though the alcoholic can become verbally or physically abusive when intoxicated. The question then becomes, "Why would that person go along with and even support such behavior?" The answer is codependency, and quite often the reason is emotional abuse.

The emotionally abused find themselves in codependent relationships because of a desire to be needed, even if the need is to provide the next drink. In addition, even though a relationship is codependent, at least it is dependent in some sense. Emotional abuse often leaves scarring on the abused's sense of value. They feel unworthy to be loved, in and of themselves. In a codependent relationship, their worth is easily defined. They are often told how important they are to that person, especially when they are providing what that person wants. To feel value, even based on inappropriate or harmful behavior, the person who has been emotionally abused will enter into or continue in an unhealthy codependent relationship.

The emotional abuser succeeds when he or she is able to replace your own control over yourself with his or her control. You no longer trust yourself but instead allow the abuser to hold undue influence over your thoughts and actions. The abuser becomes, in essence, a part of you, controlling you and how you view yourself and your world. The boundary where you start and the abuser ends is blurred.

In subsequent relationships you may find yourself completely giving in to the other person, totally submerging yourself in the other person's personality, accepting his or her view of the world and of you. Unfortunately, you may seek someone who is dominant and controlling with whom to establish a relationship. The roles in this new relationship will fit into a predictable pattern.

On the other hand, you may be extremely sensitive to anything you think seems remotely like control—even commitment. It may be difficult for you to maintain intimate relationships because the giving necessary to have intimacy may trigger a highly negative response on your part. You may feel comfortable only in a relationship in which there is a deliberate lack of commitment, having decided that no one will ever have that much control over you again.

Additionally, you may be very suspicious of anyone who seeks to get to know you in a deep, personal way. You may erect elaborate barriers to keep people out or construct tests for those who seek a relationship with you to determine their real motives.

Finally, there is a danger of becoming extremely self-absorbed. If your experience has always been that whatever you did or didn't do brought an immediate, extreme reaction, you may have concluded that the world really did, in effect, revolve around you. You may have developed the habit of analyzing everything that happens around you as it relates to you, whether it really does or not.

While these tactics helped you survive your abuse, they have left you ill-prepared to operate within healthy, positive relationships. Attempting to submerge yourself completely into a healthy relationship may make you appear possessive and clingy, suffocating the other person in your need to meld your individuality with his or hers. On the other hand, a suspicion of intimacy and a general aloofness may dissuade most others from even attempting a relationship with you. And being extremely self-absorbed leaves little room for thoughts of others.

Isolation from Others

The opposite of relationship is isolation. When a person feels inadequate to handle relationship, he or she may decide to withdraw from other people. It may appear as if the person is sinking into depression. Certainly, one of the symptoms of depression is increased isolation, but some people have been so hurt by emotionally abusive relationships that they decide not to enter into relationships at all. You may be such a person. You may deliberately live apart from extended family and experience no toll due to the loss of contact. Other people, being unsafe, are just an impediment to you. Therefore, you feel more comfortable, safer, more in control, when it is just you.

For stimulation and a feeling of connection, you may turn to coping activities, such as television, video games, and the Internet. With television, you can vicariously observe and comment on the relationships of other people, which for the purpose of dramatic tension are often tumultuous, validating your opinion that people aren't worth it. With a video game, you have the ability to become whomever you want, to assume a separate identity. With interactive, online gaming, you can actually interact with other people while keeping your anonymity intact. On the Internet, virtually anything goes.

If you want to remain anonymous and disconnected from people, you can gain more information than you could ever possibly utilize, all without having to talk to a single person. If you want to engage in interactive activities, you can enter chat rooms, game rooms, online gaming sites, each one with a different identity.

Many times emotionally abused persons will be in a relationship with another person but warily so. They may need to retreat often to an avoidance activity such as viewing television, playing video games, or going online in order to safeguard themselves against too deep an intimacy with the other person. If you are someone who feels the need to "escape" through one of these activities, you may experience a desire to spend more and more time doing one of these and feel less and less compelled to spend time with the other person in your relationship.

Remember, these activities are ultimately about control. Television sets come with a remote. Video games come with a controller. The Internet comes with a keyboard. All of these come with an off switch. People, on the other hand, do not. As such, these activities, being easier to control, may seem safer and more pleasurable to you because of the damage you have experienced through past emotionally abusive relationships.

Excessive Compliance or Passivity

While some people who have been emotionally abused will reject further relationships with people, others will crave relationships at any cost. One of the costs you may be willing to pay to be in relationship with others is becoming excessively compliant or passive in the relationship. If you have determined that the only way to be liked or accepted in the relationship is to do whatever the other person asks, you barter with compliance. The relationship is valuable to you because it validates that you are worthy of another person, in defiance of what others have told you in the past. You literally will do whatever is necessary to please the other person so that person will love you.

All of us in a loving relationship with another person strive to fill that person's needs and desires whenever possible. In a healthy relationship, one person doesn't request something of the other person that would be harmful to that person. In a healthy relationship, if that did happen, you would be able to say no. The excessively compliant will say yes even if there is a significant physical or emotional cost to doing so. And he or she will keep on saying yes, being under the impression that saying no would result in the relationship being damaged or broken.

The difficulty with excessive compliance is that it is hard to maintain for long stretches of time. Inevitably, compliance will give way to passivity. If the other person continues to ask, you may not be able to say yes, but you will avoid saying no. Instead, you will say yes but just not follow through. Compliant people have no boundaries for others. Passive people keep their boundaries hidden out of fear. Boundaries are a natural, necessary part of any relationship. Where those boundaries are depends on the nature of the relationship. Emotional abuse takes those boundaries, sucks them up like a tornado, and deposits them in odd and unusual places all over your relational landscape.

A Time to Heal

Some of the greatest damage done by emotional abuse is through the destruction not only of past relationships but also of present ones. I have found that many people do not connect their present relationship difficulties with the emotional abuse they suffered in the past. In order to move forward, it is necessary to go back and make some sense of the past. This is especially true for those who suffered emotional abuse from family members during childhood. The template of what a "normal" family or "normal relationships" looks like is skewed.

I cannot say that most people look forward to going back and reevaluating their past and their childhood, or even going back and examining a difficult relationship in the past. The strong drive to ignore, deny, and accept, which we spoke about in chapter 2, is hard to push through. But you must push through, or you will end up stuck in the cycle of perpetuation.

Let's look again at the damage done to relationships through persistent emotional abuse, as discussed in this chapter:

- distortion of what is normal, with negative consequences to all relationships
- undercutting of a strong and healthy sense of self
- establishment of a potential for emotional abuse in future relationships
- difficulty with intimacy
- caution, fear, and suspicion in relationships
- perfectionism
- feelings of abandonment
- emotional triggers of fear, guilt, and anger

- hypersensitivity
- tension and confusion in current relationships, including work relationships
- rejection of authority or need for controlling authority figures
- cycling the pattern of abuse with your own children
- codependency
- unhealthy desire to be needed
- isolation from others
- inappropriate coping activities, such as television, Internet, gaming, or food
- excessive compliance or passivity

1. In this chapter there were several vignettes, situations described to illustrate each point. Did any of these resonate with you? If so, which ones, and why?
2. In your current relationships, which effects on this list are the most pervasive?
3. What have you done in the past to try to mitigate these effects?
4. Were these efforts successful in the short term? Were they successful in the long term? Why or why not?
5. If you could remove one of these effects from your life today, how would your life be different?
6. How do you feel about relationships in general? Are you open, guarded, suspicious, impulsive, or careful? What word best describes your response to new relationships?
7. Take a moment and write down the significant relationships you currently have in your life—with yourself,

family (spouse, children, extended), friends, co-workers, those in clubs or social groups, and God.

8. Next, evaluate each relationship in regard to this list. How is each relationship doing? Where are some areas of growth?

9. Are you able to identify any relationships that need to be significantly modified—including ending them—based on their effects on you? Which ones would you modify, in what ways, and why?

10. Look at the number of relationships you wrote down. Are you surprised at how many relationships you are part of? Are you disappointed there aren't more?

11. Do you see a value for relationships in your life? If so, how do relationships add to your life? If not, why do you consider relationships of little value?

12. Ephesians 4:16 says, "From him [Christ] the whole body, joined and held together by every supporting ligament, grows and builds itself up in love, as each part does its work." Do you see yourself as part of a whole? Or are you a lone ranger?

Relationships are vital to life. You have a relationship with yourself and hopefully with others, and are created to be in relationship with God. Life is enhanced by extended relationships with family and friends. Emotional abuse short-circuits relationships by establishing unhealthy, destructive patterns. The answer to emotional abuse is not to forgo relationships but to seek to build healthy, loving relationships in which your three basic needs—to be understood, to be accepted, and to be affirmed—can be filled.

13. As you look over all your relationships, which is the most uplifting and encouraging to you? Why?

14. In which relationship are you the most uplifting and encouraging to the other person?

15. First Corinthians 13:6–7 says, "Love . . . always protects, always trusts, always hopes, always perseveres." How do the most significant relationships you have today match up with this passage?

Part 4

OVERCOMING
EMOTIONAL ABUSE

11

Recognizing Your Abuse and Its Effects

> There comes a critical time in each person's life when the truth is accessible. Faced with it, you can either run and hide, denying it, or you can face your truth, accept it, and grow stronger.

Truth doesn't stop being truth because we refuse to look at it. It simply remains an unacknowledged truth that hangs around our necks like an albatross. Far too many of us go through life trying numerous destructive ways to deny our truth. There comes a time to stop and face it.

While reading this book, you have been presented with many different ideas and a lot of information about emotional abuse. You have been able to see the effect it has had in the lives of some of the people with whom I have come into contact. You have started down a path of self-examination through the "A Time to Heal" sections. We are now going to continue that journey. As you read this chapter, continue to meditate on how it applies to you directly.

Some Assembly Required

I have found that for many people, working through overcoming their past emotional abuse is sort of like what happens just before Christmas for the parents of children. I have two small people in my house, and invariably I end up buying something that must be assembled at the last minute before it can go under the tree.

Part of me wants to avoid even purchasing That Which Must Be Assembled because of the time, energy, and frustration involved in the assembly. The other part of me looks forward to the process, arduous though it may be, because of the benefits at the end—when That Which Must Be Assembled is actually assembled and presented to the person I love so much.

In this section, your ability to recover from the past and enjoy strong, healthy relationships is That Which Must Be Assembled. The assembly itself will take time, energy, and probably a level of frustration. You may even hesitate to continue at times. But the person you love who will be presented with the finished product at the end is you, and that product will benefit all your other relationships. So I urge you to continue and not give up. This assembly is well worth it!

At the end of each chapter so far, in the "A Time to Heal" sections, there have been a series of directed questions. I sincerely hope you have been working through those as you've been reading. I hope you have been writing down your answers, impressions, questions, and thoughts. It is one thing to mentally answer a question; it is quite another to acknowledge the reality of that response in writing.

If you have not written anything down yet, don't worry—

Recognizing Your Abuse and Its Effects

you'll be given another opportunity to do so. Why? Because something as complex as That Which Must Be Assembled is generally not put together without constantly going back to the directions. Even with something as relatively simple as a child's toy, I have to repeatedly stop what I'm doing and read again how to do it right. I'll carefully read over what I'm supposed to do, and then something won't look right or work right, so I'll have to go back and read it through again. The more complicated the assembly, the more times I need to stop and refer, and the less I'll actually do between.

I've always referred to this process as "baby steps," and there is nothing childish about that. Taking baby steps is recognizing the degree of difficulty, the importance of what I'm doing, and the deep desire to do it correctly. I know that if I don't do the assembly right, it will mean going back and redoing what I've already done in order to get all the parts to fit and work right. If there's no shortcut with a child's toy, don't expect there to be a shortcut for your That Which Must Be Assembled—a healthy emotional life.

When assembling a child's toy, all the parts are loose, and you start by putting them together. However, most of us have to start at a little different place for our emotional assembly. What has happened over the years is that we have parts that shouldn't be there, parts that should be there but aren't, and parts that should be in one place but are in another. So it's necessary to do some disassembly first.

Please be aware that removing these substandard parts is going to take some work. Depending on how long they've been a part of your emotional life, they may be quite entrenched in your emotional makeup. If this task seems overwhelming, I suggest you call in reinforcements. Professional counselors and therapists are trained to help you navigate through this process. They are able to spot out-of-place parts in your life and help you find a way to disengage those parts without causing the rest to come crashing down. There is no shame in asking for help; we do it all the time in other things, from mechanics to repair people to physicians and surgeons. Your emotional health is certainly as important as your physical health and vastly more important than having your car's oil changed or having a working dishwasher. If you can call in reinforcements on those things, why not for emotional brokenness?

Ignoring, Denying, Accepting, Perpetuating

Previous chapters have shown why it has been so hard in the past to recognize your abuse for what it is. You have seen that your life pattern, your family, your society, and even your historical culture all have conspired to mask the terrible truth about the effects of emotional abuse. You have seen the way you have been conditioned to ignore the emotional abuse around you. Its sheer prevalence inundates your senses, forcing you to relegate it to the position of background noise in your life.

When you could no longer ignore its existence, you learned to deny its ill effects. You went out of your way to justify your abusers, convincing yourself that they had a right to treat you the way they did. Numbing the pain, you stubbornly clung to the illusion that "sticks and stones may break my bones, but words can never hurt me!"

But ignoring your abuse didn't work, and denying its damage was sometimes impossible, so you learned to accept it as a part of your life—unchangeable. It became a fact of life—something that had to be dealt with stoically and survived with a minimal amount of pain. Finally, because you tried to ignore it, sought to deny it, and learned to accept it as a normal part of life, you were left with nothing else but to perpetuate it and its effects in your own life and relationships.

You should not beat yourself up because you didn't see it sooner. There are valid reasons why recognizing your abuse was extremely difficult. Instead, you should be applauding your vision, your ability to see through all of the smoke screens sent up by these powerful influences. You have seen through to the truth about emotional abuse in general and are ready to accept the truth of your own abuse in particular.

Ignoring, denying, and accepting emotional abuse and its effects in your life are part of your assembly that need to be discarded. Out of sheer desperation and need in the past, you have used them to jury-rig your emotional health. In order to make your assembly sound and fit, these odd-shaped and inferior parts need to be jettisoned. Otherwise your emotional health will not be strong as it is reassembled.

Recognizing Your Emotional Damage

As you begin to take a hard look at your own personal history of abuse and abusive relationships, you will have a natural tendency to want to minimize the horror of what has happened to you. Reluctant to relive the pain, your mind will try to convince you that what you remember wasn't so bad.

It is important at this time to take a moment and remind yourself of just how damaging emotional abuse really is. You will be fighting against the repeated, implanted messages that were programmed into you by those who abused you and by society at large. You must fight those messages by accepting the truth of the pain you feel.

Remember also how damaging the emotions are that emotional abuse triggers: fear, guilt, and anger. Other damaging emotions caused by emotional abuse fall under these main categories. Think back to how it felt for you when you were in the midst of being abused, how you felt after the abuse was over, and how much you feared for the abuse to start all over again. When the messages from the past try to tell you you're "making a mountain out of a molehill," remember the feelings you had while toiling up that "molehill."

Again, I urge you to obtain the direction and help of a professional counselor or therapist if you feel overwhelmed with the thought of recognizing your pain. Your assembly may need to take place initially with a professional who can assist you to find a place of safety in which to do this work. You do not have to "do it yourself" for your work to be meaningful and valid. Some of you may be able to work through your pain with a supportive spouse or friend, but this is by no means the route everyone can or should go. If you feel the need for professional support, ask for it! (See the contact information for The Center at the back of this book.)

Recognizing the Abuser

At this point it would be helpful to review the specific types of abusers talked about in chapters 4 through 6. Be aware that as you've been thinking about these things, additional details, thoughts, and memories may surface. As you read through the types again, think about people you have had contact with in the past or present who fit each mold. These are individuals you will need to be very careful in dealing with in the future, even avoiding them if necessary. They have the potential to become toxic people in your life. Be aware also of patterns of people in your past and present, as this could be an indication of where you are perpetuating past abuse through present relationships.

Emotional Abuse through Words

The Overbearing Opinion. This person has a consistent pattern of refusing to consider your opinion and forcing you to always accept his or hers.

The Person Who Is Always Right. Whenever there is a disagreement of any sort, this person has to be right and have the last say.

The Judge and Jury. This is anyone who incorporates harsh judgments of you as a person or of your behavior as a way to control you by producing personal shame and guilt.

The Put-Down Artist. This person uses comments like "You're crazy! How could anyone think such a stupid thing?" to devalue your decisions and feelings.

The Stand-Up Comic. This person uses sarcasm to dig up past issues, drive home a point of view, or belittle you as an individual.

The Great Guilt-Giver. This person uses unrealistic and undeserved false guilt to control your behavior.

The Preacher. This person controls you through his or her "way with words" and has a sermon for every situation, especially for pointing out even the smallest faults.

The Historian. This person tells you that you are forgiven but then proceeds to bring up over and over again every past issue to shame you into accepting his or her decisions and feelings.

The Silent Treatment Abuser. This person uses the absence of words and interaction to punish and control.

Emotional Abuse through Actions

The Commander in Chief. This person desires to control every aspect of your life—from your thoughts to your actions—by rigid, militaristic behavior and expectations.

The Ventaholic. This is the person who uses screaming and name-calling as weapons to control you.

The Intimidator. This person uses intimidation, fear, anger, and inappropriate threats to get his or her way.

The Roller Coaster. This person's moods and behavior swing from one extreme to another, removing any sense of safety and consistency from your relationship.

The Dr. Jekyll and Mr. Hyde. This person has a public persona and a private persona that are distinctly different from each other, with the public persona using a false front to mask his or her true nature.

The Illusionist. The illusionist is adept at creating and projecting a false reality and uses his or her charm and charisma to deflect the truth.

The Person Who Plays Favorites. This person displays the "Why can't you be more like . . . ?" favoritism, making it clear that you do not measure up to the other child.

The Role Reverser. This type of abuser confuses and reverses relational roles, taking the role of child and leaving the child to assume the responsibilities of the parent or to serve in the role of emotional spouse.

The Empty Promiser. This person makes promises he or she has little intention of keeping. The promise is kept only if it's convenient or will bring some level of gain. His or her word is only that, without security or substance.

The Wrath-of-God Abuser. This person misuses Scripture to get his or her own way and equates his or her own opinion with that of God.

Emotional Abuse through Neglect

The MIA Parent. This parent *physically* removes himself or herself from any interaction in your life.

The Distant Caregiver. This parent removes himself or herself *emotionally* from interaction in your life.

The Emotionally Detached Parent. This parent provides for the physical needs of life but chooses to place his or her priorities somewhere other than on you.

By this time you probably have already identified who these people are, through personal reflection and the "A Time to Heal" sections. As you have read over the examples, you probably have also relived some of the emotions you associate with these people. It would be easier at this point to say everything has been done, that as long as you have identified your abusers, you are now free to go on with your life, vowing never to have anything to do with them again. But recognizing your abusers is only the beginning step to recognizing the long-term effects of their abuse.

Recognizing the Effect on You

Because your abuse was part of your past, it has contaminated your present self. You must deal with yourself and the effect your abuse has on past, present, and future relationships.

In chapter 8, I discussed the ways I have seen abuse affect people I have worked with. Take some time to rethink them. Discover whether you feel you have been affected in ways I haven't mentioned. Each person is unique. While the effects may be similar, they need not be identical.

low self-esteem	perfectionism
lack of self-confidence	unrealistic guilt
transfer of needs	crisis oriented
acting out sexually	unresolved anger and
loneliness	resentments
failure syndrome	

I'm sure you can add one or more of your own effects of abuse after thinking about that list. Just because something unique to you isn't listed doesn't mean the effect isn't valid. These are presented to you as frameworks within which you can explore the effects of your own abuse.

Go back through the questions at the end of chapter 8 and your responses to them. If you haven't yet worked through this chapter, please do so now. Then come back and highlight those areas you have pinpointed as areas for deeper evaluation and recovery.

Recognizing the Effects on Your Health

Your emotions don't operate within a vacuum. The emotional delivery system is chemical- and body-based. What your mind feels, your body experiences.

Over the years you may have developed chronic health problems that seem impervious to medical treatment. Doctors may have shaken their heads and muttered under their breath that they could find nothing wrong with you. In reviewing the list of physical reactions I gave in chapter 9, think about your own state of health and how the emotional abuse in your past may have contributed to ongoing physical conditions you are facing now.

addictions	eating disorders
allergies/asthma	hypochondria
depression	chronic fatigue syndrome
anxiety	migraine headaches
digestive disturbances	panic attacks

phobias   unexplained physical pain
unexplained skin rashes

In no way am I trying to say that every physical problem you may be currently facing is a direct result of the emotional abuse you have suffered. However, if you have hard-to-explain, chronic problems that have defied treatment, maybe it's time to look for more than just an organic source.

At The Center, we utilize a medical team that includes a medical doctor, a psychiatrist, a naturopathic physician, and registered dietitians. Over the years, many people have come to us for help after years of unsuccessful treatment by traditional medical providers. They are tired of popping pills without getting any better. Concerned about the long-term side effects of the pharmaceuticals they're taking, they want to experience results with the lowest possible dose. They also want to explore, with medical direction, alternative or holistic approaches to wellness. Because we address the whole person, our medical team is acutely aware of how emotional issues relate to physical symptoms and conditions.

We certainly recognize the trust relationship that exists between a person and his or her doctor. When individuals come to work with us in our intensive recovery programs, we cooperate and coordinate our efforts for their benefit. Some people, however, come to recognize that they have neglected an aspect of medical care—either alternative or traditional—that could provide relief and recovery from their physical conditions.

As you are in the process of evaluating the effects of past emotional abuse on your physical health, please also evaluate the effectiveness of care you've been receiving. More and more, people are recognizing that it may take a team of medical professionals working together to assist in recovery—medical, naturopathic, and nutritional. This is a powerful recovery triad, one we see producing amazing results for those who come to us for help at The Center.

Recognizing the Effects of Negative Emotionality

Past negative messages can affect you in several different ways. Those messages of failure and inadequacy may cause you never to attempt to do or achieve anything. You may have developed a dependency on others to carry out routine tasks. The very thought of attempting to achieve something noteworthy or special may cause an immediate panic reaction of *What am I even thinking of? I could never do that!* And so, of course, you don't. The fear of failure is so great that you become paralyzed and achieve very little, further substantiating the messages that say, "You're nothing."

The opposite reaction of doing nothing is attempting to do everything. I have found that most often the tendency toward perfection is driven by a series of messages given to an individual that "motivates" his or her desire to be perfect. Stated and implied messages, such as "You're not good enough, thin enough, smart enough, strong enough . . . ," are replayed over and over in the back of your mind. They can warp your view of yourself, sap emotional energy, and drive you to constantly prove those messages wrong by engaging in superhuman feats of effort and stamina.

In order to determine what those messages are, you need to first evaluate how you feel about yourself. Emotional abuse tears at a person's sense of self-worth. The verbal and non-verbal messages conveyed through emotional abuse are like tapes that are played over and over in our minds. "I'm not worth anything" or "I'll never be able to do that" aren't generally assumptions we have come to on our own. We have been "helped" along the way by the opinions of others transferred to us through their words and actions.

I realize we're not to the end of the chapter yet, but this is so important that I'd like you to take a moment and do the following exercise. Below, write down five things you feel about yourself. Try to use single words or short phrases to describe what you think about yourself and what sort of person you are. This isn't how you want to be or think you should be, but how you are today.

I am:

1. _____
2. _____
3. _____
4. _____
5. _____

Next, write down five goals you have for yourself. Again, try to use single words or short phrases.

My goals are:

1. _____
2. _____
3. _____
4. _____
5. _____

Looking at each characteristic or description of yourself, think about when you first came to feel that way. Is this an opinion you came to on your own? Did you hear or feel it from someone else? Who? Write down the origin of your opinion. (Also write down the first thoughts that come to mind. Don't talk yourself out of whatever your answer is. No matter how odd or far-fetched your recollection seems, go ahead and write it down.)

Look at your goals. How long have you had them? When do you first remember having them as goals? Do you remember who first came up with the goals? Was it you or someone else? If someone else, who gave each goal to you? If they did not originate with you, do you still want to claim them as your own?

Next to each goal, write either "claim" or "discharge." If you determine to discharge a goal, do you have a personal goal—one of your own choosing—you'd like to replace it with? If so, write it down.

Look back over what you have written. How many positive characteristics did you list? How many negative? What about your goals? How realistic are they? The more perfectionistic you are, the more negative and unrealistic your lists. While the normal person will be able to see both good and bad qualities, the person who has suffered emotional abuse will often see an overbalance of negative traits. In addition, perfectionism pushes for unrealistic, unclaimed goals.

As you identify these negative messages and where they came from, you can begin to erase them from the tape recorder that is your subconscious mind. This is part of the important work of disassembly that must take place to recapture a healthy emotional life. You erase negative messages by seeing them for what they are and by identifying their origin. Many of them have to do with who you were, not who you are. As we grow up, we change and make progress in our thinking and behaviors. As we pass from childhood into adulthood, we may need to reevaluate those messages and hear them as the adults we are, not as the children we were.

But often it is not enough just to erase the old messages; they have the ability to come back when least expected or desired. To ensure that negative messages are permanently erased, it will be necessary to record over them with positive messages of self-worth and acceptance. It is important that these messages come first from you.

There are a variety of ways to reassemble your life with positive messages about yourself. Place words and phrases of personal affirmation where you will see them often (refrigerator, work desk, bedroom or bathroom mirror). I've seen people use brightly colored paper, Post-it notes, and pens to decorate and emphasize the positive nature of the messages. Reward yourself on a regular basis with something you have decided reinforces your worthiness (fresh flowers on your desk, a new haircut, a routine walk in the park). At first this might seem awkward or contrived; that's because it is. The messages in your mind are like whispers of background noise. Sometimes you will need to drown them out with something you can see, hear, or touch. Whenever you see it or do it, you will be reminded that you are a special person.

Another way to record positive messages is through the appreciation of other people. Try joining a service club or church. Focusing on and helping others provides a needed break and a new perspective on our own problems. And besides, service groups are notorious for needing help! They are usually highly appreciative of those who take the time to volunteer. If you are hesitant to try something new, remember that most groups will extend extra patience for anyone willing to volunteer time and energy. Let their appreciation for your efforts help record over some of your negative messages.

Another important way to build up your self-esteem and tear down negative messages is to surround yourself with positive people. Of course, the first person to surround yourself with is . . . you. Make an effort to be positive and encouraging and to forgive yourself. Then look for others who make you feel good about yourself, who appreciate you for who you are.

Since nobody is perfect, the negative messages will resurface from time to time, probably when you are in a stressful situation. This is normal. They were recorded under stressful situations, and those are the times that are most likely to bring them out. So don't be surprised; be prepared. Be prepared to put your present stressful situation into perspective without bringing up the tapes of the past. Turn up those positive messages *full blast*!

Recognizing the Effects on Relationships

As we have seen, perhaps one of the most important truths for you to recognize if you have been emotionally abused is that in most cases your abuse will have adversely affected the way you view yourself. It will be necessary to go back through your mind and replay those negative messages associated with your abuse, realize they were false messages, and start rerecording positive, uplifting, life-changing messages of your own.

In addition, if you are in a long-term or permanent relationship with another person, you will need to ascertain just how this relationship is being adversely affected by your abuse and your past and present response to that abuse.

In chapter 10, I reviewed several of the difficulties in relationships that I have seen in working with those who have been emotionally abused. An honest evaluation of whether emotional abuse has hindered past relationships, is hindering present relationships, or might hinder future relationships is necessary to being able to develop and maintain the kind of healthy interaction so necessary to communication and growth in relationships.

lack of intimate relationships

codependency

inappropriate relationships

isolation from others

excessive compliance or passivity

One of those problems may be in experiencing and maintaining a necessary sense of intimacy with your sexual partner. It is difficult to totally relax around another person if we are constantly on guard.

Overcoming a fear of sexual intimacy will take time and patience. Identifying why being with another person is frightening or uncomfortable for you is essential. If your partner is willing to discuss such a sensitive subject with you, you can talk together about your sexual experiences and how you feel about them. Initially, it would be helpful if these discussions could stand on their own, without the expectation that they will lead to sexual intimacy. Without the pressure to perform, you both may be able to relax and be more open about how you feel.

Sometimes it is good, when dealing with such a charged subject, to obtain professional help. Talking to a third party or having a third party present can help diffuse tension. A counselor or health professional also can be helpful in knowing which questions to ask and in providing physical or anatomical information that you may not have access to.

As your acceptance of yourself grows, as you rerecord positive messages about yourself, as you learn to relax around yourself and enjoy who you are, your ability to relax around others will increase. Much of the fulfillment of sexual intimacy has to do with relaxing and enjoying yourself, your partner, and the experience itself.[1]

Another thing that may contaminate your current relationships is the desire for perfection. Letting go of your own need to be perfect will allow you to release your rigid control over your environment and those in it. Understand that it is normal and realistic for people, even yourself, to make mistakes. Be gentle and forgiving with yourself when you fall short. Remember the positive things about yourself. Learn to laugh at your mistakes and move on.

We must see ourselves from the proper perspective. No one is perfect. No one can be perfect. All we can do is our best, whatever that means for each person. Each of us needs to be given a break, to be allowed to be human. When we are happy with ourselves and at ease with where we are and where we are going, we can relax around others. We no longer see them as obstacles to our perfect goals that we must maneuver around, or as walking, talking pawns to be moved at our will on the chessboard of our lives.

Anger, fear, and guilt are powerful emotions. If you were abused as a child, these emotions were an essential part of growing up. Your abuse intensified them, and you were left with no healthy model of how to cope with these emotions. You will need to recognize the ways in which you are still trying to deal with the anger, fear, and guilt left over from your abusive relationships.

Any part of your body that gets hit over and over again becomes sensitive. Even though a callus might form, you still will experience immediate and intense pain if it is hit in the right spot. Within relationships, your abuse has left you with several sensitive spots. If they are touched, even if not by the person who did most of the damage, you will hurt. When you are hurt, you may react with anger, fear, or feelings of guilt. You may explode in anger one day over some inconsequential incident. The person who set you off might not even understand what he or she has done, and certainly not why you are acting in such an odd way.

A casual comment at work could lead you to fear whether your employer or co-worker likes you or thinks you are doing a good job. Or the same comment could cause you to negatively reevaluate your work performance and feel guilty for some "error" on your part. Again, you need to gain a sense of perspective and try to identify why what was done produced such a reaction. If possible, try to remember other times in your life when you felt the same way. Determine whether the anger, fear, or guilt you feel is really related to the current situation or is a holdover from some past incident.

Nearly everyone will blow up in anger over something little—whether it's the guy who cut you off on the freeway, the busy signal you always seem to get when you call a certain number, or the waitress who gave you cream in your coffee instead of leaving it black. Pile up enough of those annoyances, and most people will need to let off steam. But if the explosion of steam is wildly out of proportion, or if you find the anger, fear, or guilt doesn't subside as quickly as it came, then it's time to find yourself a quiet place and think about why you are feeling the way you are. If you can't come up with an answer or if this seems to happen too often, finding someone to talk with would be very helpful.

You may use your existing friendships as a filter through which to see these outbursts. Talking to a friend about the incident may help you decide if you were out of line or inappropriate in your reaction. Good and trusted friends are a wonderful resource for helping you gauge your reactions. There are times, however, when talking to a friend may bring understanding but not the tools you need to change your behavior. At that point you may need more than a friend to talk to. You may want to seek out professional counseling.

If you hold down a job outside your home, you will by necessity develop relationships at work, and these relationships will not be immune to the effects of your abuse. Emotional abuse can damage all your relationships. Be aware of feeling inadequate on the job, of feeling that somehow the good things that are happening in your career are undeserved, or of looking at your work relationships through the lens of familial ones in which a boss becomes father, a supervisor becomes mother, or a co-worker becomes sibling. When this situation arises, you have a couple of choices. The obvious one is to find another job. However, that may not solve the problem. You may find yourself feeling the same way in another position with another person.

The other choice is to stay where you are and deal with the way you feel about this person. Try doing what I call a reality check. If your employer calls you into his office to talk about something, say to yourself before you open the door, "He is not my father. He's just my boss." If your supervisor criticizes some piece of work, remind yourself after she has left, "She is not my mother, and I am no longer a child." If a co-worker begins to expect you to do too many favors or cover for him at work, tell yourself, "We are both employees. He is not my brother, and I don't need to make up excuses for him. It's not fair to myself or my employer."

Maintaining a sense of present-day reality on the job can go a long way in helping you deal with individuals whose personalities seem to correspond with past relationships. Getting to know the person you are having a problem relating to can also help solidify that person's own identity in your mind. The better you know the person, the less like someone else he or she may seem.

Finally, when looking at your relationships, don't forget your spiritual nature. This is a vital aspect of your whole person. Your relationship with God can help you define who you are, why you are here, and where you are going. If you have a tendency to view God as a stern, unforgiving "superparent," the relationship you have with him will be nothing more than an enlarged copy of your relationship with the parent who abused you. Your spiritual relationship should offer you comfort, peace, and security, not a supernaturally motivated repeat of anger, fear, and guilt.

To change your perception of God as unforgiving, you could start with two things. First, try reading the Bible. It is amazing how many people who profess to follow it haven't actually read it for themselves! This time, read it without anyone else telling you what God says or demands. Allow God to reveal himself through his words to you personally, unfiltered by another's perspective or bias. Seek to develop your own relationship with him. Let him speak to you directly, not through someone else. Try underlining all the places where his grace, mercy, and forgiveness are shown or promised.

Second, observe the people around you in your religious setting. If they, for the most part, reinforce this vision of the stern, unforgiving God, it might be wise to seek out another group. Find one in which God's grace and forgiveness are emphasized. Before you become fully involved in a religious body, set up an appointment with one of the leaders and find out how they view God. If it's too much like the harsh view you grew up with, seek somewhere else with God's help.

Recognizing Your Abuse through Your Children

Nothing seems to put people into better contact with their parents than becoming a parent themselves. If your abuser was your mother or your father, becoming a parent yourself will undoubtedly bring up the memory of that past abuse. Either you will attempt to scrupulously avoid any hint of abuse, swinging to the side of overprotectionism, or you will find yourself coming full circle by abusing your own children as you were abused. This is one of the most difficult truths you will have to face. Please don't turn away from it. There is too much at stake.

Because so much is involved, I cannot urge you enough to immediately seek professional counseling for your situation. This is a time when I say, don't walk—*run* to the nearest help. I wish insurance carriers covered mental health services in proportion to medical services, but the sad fact is, most don't. You may find you're on your own as far as paying for professional counseling. Many places, like The Center, operate with a sliding fee scale for services. There are also some governmental or religious organizations that assist with counseling services. Whatever the case, if you need professional help, be as creative as possible to get it. I am amazed at how much money people will spend on junk food, cigarettes, alcohol, and caffeinated products weekly, if not daily, yet somehow they can't find the money to get professional help. If this is a priority for your life and your family, find a way. Your entire family can benefit greatly from professional help.

Now is the time to stand up and say, "I'm going to put an end to this cycle of abuse. I need help to deal with my own abuse, and I need help not to be an abuser myself." With a professional to guide you, you can work toward a healthy parenting style, one that neither overdisciplines with harshness and abuse nor underdisciplines by failing to provide needed boundaries for the child. With proper guidance, your family can find a healthy, happy medium. That is what you so desperately needed and wanted as a child. Now it's time to give that to your own children and to yourself.

If your current assembly includes parts handed down to you by those who abused you, and you find yourself using them on your own children, it's time to do the work to disassemble that model and remove those parts. The perpetuation of the emotional abuse you suffered can truly end with you.

A Time to Heal

You are a person who is connected to others through a web of personal and spiritual relationships. Emotional, physical, spiritual, relational—your whole person. To deny one aspect of yourself is to blind yourself to the interdependency of these different aspects. The effects of emotional abuse can damage all of these areas. Healing only part of your whole person still leaves part that is wounded.

Healing the whole person is possible. It happens when you get over the past and start living for the future. Now is the time to face up to your truth and begin.

There are some excellent ways that you can start to heal from the damage of abuse and reconstruct a life of optimism, hope, and joy. Through intentionally choosing how to react to life, you can detach yourself from the automatic reactions that have built up because of your past.

Choose to respond to situations instead of react. If your normal reactions stem from negative feelings and experiences, your immediate reactions will be negative also. Choose instead to determine how you are going to respond. Give yourself a moment to acknowledge your reaction, but take control over your response. Stop and think what you want your response to reflect about who you are as a person. Take back control through your response.

1. Think back over the recent past. Was there an instance where you reacted disproportionately in a significantly negative way to events or circumstances? Write down how you reacted.

2. Why did you react that way? Can you remember if anything else was going through your mind at the time?

3. If there was another person involved, did the other person appear surprised by your reaction?

4. Whether or not another person was involved, as you look back at what happened, do you regret how you reacted?

5. How do you normally react to difficult or stressful situations? Are there situations where you automatically seem to react with anger, indifference, or sarcasm?

6. How do you feel when you react in this way? Does it feel like the anger, indifference, or sarcasm buffers you from the difficult or stressful situation?

7. Could you have responded to what happened in a different way? Could you have responded more positively?

8. If you had responded in a different way, what do you think the outcome would have been?

9. At what point in the event could you have taken control and responded instead of reacted?

10. If a similar situation arises in the future, what can you do to avoid merely reacting and instead respond intentionally in a better way?

11. Write down some positive reasons why responding is better than reacting. Below are some of mine. You are welcome to adopt these as your own or come up with additional ones.

   • Responding instead of reacting to people and events allows you to have control over the situation.

- Responding instead of reacting allows you to be alert when old reactions attempt to take control of current events.
- Responding instead of reacting gives you greater choice in how to handle difficult or stressful situations.
- Responding instead of reacting reinforces who you choose to be rather than trapping you within the reactions of your past.

Accept your own response without needing approval from others. If you have grown up with emotional abuse, you may have learned to distrust your responses. Choose to trust in your ability to make appropriate judgments regarding responses to situations in your life. If others approve of your decisions, that is certainly fine. But ultimately you are the one who has to live with those responses. Make the best decisions you can and be proud of yourself. Don't wait for the approval of others, which may not come.

1. Do you find you wait to see how other people react in situations before you respond?
2. Do you distrust your own decisions and opinions? If so, in all situations or just certain situations? Which ones?
3. Do you feel you are able to make good judgments about situations you face in life?
4. When was the last time you made a good judgment? What was it?
5. When was the last time you made a bad judgment? What was it?

6. Was it easier to come up with an example of a bad judgment than a good judgment? If so, why do you suppose that is?

7. After you make a bad judgment, what do you tell yourself?

8. After you make a good judgment, what do you tell yourself?

9. After you've made a bad judgment, are you able to forgive yourself? If so, why? If not, why not?

10. Do you seek out the approval of others to feel better about your responses to situations?

11. Do you second-guess yourself and worry over how you responded?

Realize that it will take time for you to become comfortable responding to life and its situations on your own. This is part of the maturation process that was circumvented by the emotional abuse you suffered. Often the abuse was used specifically to prevent you from growing up and becoming an independent person in your own right. So expect your responses to life to feel a little strange, even a little scary, at first. The more comfortable you become with yourself, the easier they will become. You'll learn to trust yourself and your responses with each right decision. You'll learn to forgive yourself, learn, and move on with each wrong decision.

Allow others to make their own decisions. One of the most common forms of compensation used by those who have been emotionally abused as children is an inappropriate need for control in life as adults. Having felt out of control and powerless as a child, as an adult you cling to control as a way to feel safe. This death grip on control ends up strangling present relationships. To heal, you must loosen your need to control your circumstances and those around you. Just as you need to feel complete without the approval of others, you also need others to act without requiring approval from you.

Because this need for control can be so pervasive, it can also become almost invisible to the person needing the control and normal for those in close relationship. Think about how you would react in the following situation.

You are part of a group of people (say, twelve to fifteen) involved in a decision-making process. The decision you're working toward is an important one and will affect many people, including yourself. Although there is a leader of the group, the structure is very loose, and everyone is encouraged to participate and provide opinions and direction.

1. Given the parameters of this group, are you confident such a configuration can result in positive action?
2. Are you confident such a configuration can result in time-efficient action?
3. If the flow of the group process starts to wander, would you feel compelled to put things "back on track"?
4. If a majority of the group appeared to be coming to a consensus and it wasn't your top choice, how strongly would you object?
5. If decisions did not happen in a time-efficient manner, would you continue to be part of the group?

Now I'd like you to think about some other groups you are part of and how you interact with those groups.

6. When you are with a group of friends, how often do you speak up? If there are five people in the group, do you speak around 20 percent of the time? Do you speak more or less?

7. If your family decided to go out to dinner, how often is your restaurant preference chosen?

8. If your restaurant preference is not chosen, is it difficult for you to enjoy your meal?

9. Do you express your opinion to others about what they should wear, how they should wear their hair, where they should shop, or what they should buy, even if you're not specifically asked?

10. Do other people consider you to be opinionated?

11. Are you more comfortable making a decision than following the decisions of others?

12. Will you follow the decision of another even if you don't agree with it?

13. Do you feel more comfortable being a leader or a follower?

14. Do you feel more comfortable in a group of people when you know what to expect?

15. How do you react when another person disagrees with you about something important to you?

16. Do you generally feel your decisions are right and appropriate for everyone involved?

All of us have a perception about the world around us. We make decisions based on this perception. The danger can occur when we begin to feel that our view of the world and how it works is the *only* correct view. This danger springs from a compelling need for control. I have seen this in adult children of alcoholics—their home life was chaotic due to an alcoholic parent.

I have also seen this need for control as a result of emotional abuse. Anytime the decisions of others have the potential to do harm or cause injury to a person, he or she may grasp tightly to the reigns of control over self and anyone else in relationship. Letting go of that control allows other people to relax and be who they are.

Utilize the power of forgiveness liberally. Evil, destructive people must be scrupulously avoided. Everyone else, including yourself, requires a lot of forgiveness. You cannot punish your abuser by withholding forgiveness from others. On the contrary, you can repudiate your abuser and supersede the abuse by intentionally choosing to live a different type of life, with positive responses. Of all of the ways we can respond to each other, you can choose love, mercy, and forgiveness. These will first enrich your life, then bless the lives of others.

We'll talk more about forgiveness in the next chapter, but I want you to think about what forgiveness means to you.

1. Does forgiveness mean letting someone off the hook?
2. It has been said that forgiving is also forgetting. Do you believe that's a good definition? If so, why? If not, why not?
3. Is it difficult for you to grant someone forgiveness if he or she doesn't ask for it first?
4. Do you think forgiveness involves an element of risk? If so, what is the risk?

5. How many times should you be expected to forgive someone?

6. Are there some people you should not be expected to forgive?

7. Do you feel forgiven by God?

Stay close to God. With negative, destructive examples in your past, it is imperative that you constantly align yourself with God's overwhelmingly positive presence in your present and future. He will be your source of healing, forgiveness, and strength to rise above what was done to you by the sin of others. Even more, it is his divine desire to heal your broken heart and rebuild your damaged spirit. Make your relationship with him the primary relationship in your life. Do this, and your ability to love yourself and others will multiply in the bounty of his love for you.

We'll talk more about God and his power to help and heal in chapter 12. Until then, please take some time to think about and answer the questions below. They aren't necessarily meant to draw you into a conclusion but are meant to stimulate thought as we continue through this chapter and the rest of this section.

1. How would you describe your present relationship with God?

2. Are you satisfied with your present relationship with God? If so, why? If not, why not?

3. Do you feel comfortable praying to God by yourself? When you pray to God, do you feel close to him?

4. Do you pray because you want to talk to God or because you feel obligated to?

5. Does the thought of praying make you fearful, uncomfortable, awkward, or apprehensive?

6. How often do you pray? Do you feel this is enough? If it's not enough, do you feel guilty for not praying more?

7. Do you spend time regularly reading God's Word? Do you generally understand what you read?

8. Have you ever felt God speak to you through what you read? If so, in what way?

9. Do you read the Bible out of a sense of obligation or duty?

10. Do you feel the Bible is relevant and meaningful for you today? If not, why not?

11. Do you often feel distant or isolated from God?

12. Are you a member of a faith community? If so, what do you gain from being a member?

13. If you are not a member of a faith community, what reasons have you given for not joining?

14. If you are a member of a faith community, are you as involved and active as you think you should be? If so, what are you doing?

15. If you are not as involved and active as you think you should be, can you identify the barriers that hold you back?

God, with your love to strengthen me, I can truly look at and understand how I have been hurt. Bind my wounds. Rebuild who you created me to be. Help me trust you. Help me to forgive myself and others.

12

Getting Over the Past and Living for the Future

> "For I know the plans I have for you," declares the LORD, "plans to prosper you and not to harm you, plans to give you hope and a future."
>
> Jeremiah 29:11

"Did you take that dress back to the store today?" A simple question, spoken quietly. Someone passing by probably would think nothing of this ordinary inquiry from a husband to a wife.

Paul and Sarah were out for a walk around the lake. A time to discuss the bits and pieces of the day. A time to relax and reconnect after a busy week. "Did you take that dress back to the store today?" Paul asked.

A year earlier Paul either would not have had the courage to ask that question or would have already known the answer. The answer, of course, would have been "No."

Back then, Sarah never took anything back to a store. Not to a clothing store or a grocery store or any kind of store. No matter if the milk was sour or the dress didn't fit or the printer cartridge was the wrong type. It had taken him about a year into their marriage to realize this aspect of his new wife. He began to recognize other things too. Like Sarah's difficulty making decisions without him. Her need to keep everything around the house in perfect order. Her overreacting with tears to things he said or did. Finding money missing from his wallet. Her behavior didn't add up. After about a year and a half of marriage, Paul decided to find out what was going on with Sarah and why she was acting this way.

Paul thought he had married an adult woman. And he had. But he came to realize that inside his beautiful adult wife were the remnants of a hurt, emotionally abused child. Even now he had to control himself as he thought about how his wife had been treated growing up. No wonder she had kept that part of herself carefully hidden from him during their dating and engagement stages. Sarah was deeply ashamed of her childhood and blamed herself for the abuse she had suffered. It made him love her even more and made him commit to helping her understand her true worth. She had been doing that through counseling, with his support, for the past year.

Paul learned that Sarah couldn't make decisions because she didn't trust her own judgment. She had worked herself ragged cleaning the house and keeping everything in place because of her fear of punishment if she wasn't perfect. Paul came to understand her emotional sensitivity at a careless word or action from him, being so sure that at any moment he would leave her. Sarah stole money from him because she didn't think he would ever give her any. It had taken Sarah a year to learn to trust herself and to trust her relationship with Paul.

The question about the dress wasn't an ordinary one; it was pivotal to her ongoing emotional restoration. Sarah looked over at him and smiled. He had specifically chosen the time and place to ask her the question, and she knew it. She was coming to know him better each day, accepting him for who he was instead of projecting onto him the harsh image of her father. Taking a deep breath, drinking in the serenity of the lake, fingers curled around his warm, strong hand, Sarah answered, "I was able to take it back today."

His fingers tightened. "That's great! I'm so proud of you. Did everything go okay?"

"It wasn't as bad as I thought," Sarah admitted. "The woman at the register was really nice. And I did have the receipt." Sarah seemed at peace, matching him stride for stride. "She put through a credit on the Visa. It went fine."

Paul raised up their joined hands and gently kissed hers. Such a seemingly small thing—being able to look a stranger in the eye and say there was something wrong with what she had bought and she would like her money back. Most people do it all the time. Sarah hadn't been able to do it before that day. She was making progress. They were making progress.

As Sarah talked with Paul, she felt like another weight had been lifted off her. Each step she took toward reconciling with the past advanced her journey into a hope-filled future. A year earlier she hadn't known that she had the courage to come out from under the shadow of her past. But she did; she was getting stronger all the time. And the most amazing thing was that she wasn't doing this for Paul; she was doing it for Sarah.

Of all the chapters in this book, this is one I have longed to share since I began writing. This is one centered on hope—that says healing is possible! Granted, it will take courage to heal. But having courage to face difficult issues will result in hope. Hope opens up the heart to change. Where change is present, healing can begin. It is possible to get over a past in which you suffered abuse and begin to really live for the future. In this chapter we are going to talk about specific ways to help you do just that. Much of the work to be done can be accomplished only by you, either by working alone or with the guidance of a trained professional. If you have a friend who has the appropriate skills to help you, that's great. Use whichever situation feels most comfortable. Whatever it takes to get on with your life, do it.

Getting on with your life means putting those feelings of anger, fear, and guilt into perspective. In this chapter we will talk about how to get beyond your anger by stepping out of the blame mode and learning how to grant forgiveness. We will look into how to banish the fear and guilt you have been feeling and reclaim your personal power.

This chapter will also give you some practical solutions for handling future conflicts. You will learn nine helpful steps you can use to combat negative emotions when someone hurts you. You will discover ways to find and maintain proper relationships with others and learn the traits of a healthy communicator. I will give you some characteristics of healthy problem solvers. I also want you to start thinking about your own gifts and talents that you may have buried. Finally, I will go over how to recognize progress in your own healing process.

Over the years I have learned that there are several things people can do to help themselves along in the healing process. In this chapter we will discuss:

- how to step out of the blame mode so common in abuse
- how to grant forgiveness, and why forgiveness is vital to healing
- how to reclaim your personal power
- how commonsense solutions can help avoid future conflicts
- nine steps to take when someone hurts you
- how to find and maintain healthy relationships
- traits of a healthy communicator
- how to discover your own gifts and talents
- characteristics of a healthy problem solver
- how to recognize progress in your own healing

Stepping out of the Blame Mode

After years of living with false guilt, fear, and repressed anger, it is common to unleash a torrent of rage and regret at what has happened to you. The tears of anger and sorrow intermix as the truth is faced. After all that has been said and done to deny the truth of your abuse, when it finally is faced, it hurts. The fresh pain produces even more anger.

Anger can be a cleansing emotion. It is focused and intense. It has a way of motivating normally uncomfortable actions. When we are angry, we are apt to do things we would never consider doing otherwise. Anger is powerful. It can make us feel strong and invincible.

Because anger is so focused, its beam is narrow.

Because anger is so intense, it needs fuel to burn.

Because anger is so powerful, it can become addictive.

When dealing with your emotional abuse, it may be easy to view things with tunnel vision. All you may see is the pain and damage of the abuse. You may not see some of the reasons behind it. Nothing can explain it away.

Some people have the distinct misfortune of coming into contact with truly evil people who abuse them in terrible ways. Most of the rest of you have been abused by people who meant better than what they did, who tried less than what they should, who should have known better but didn't.

If you were abused by your parent, one reason behind the abuse may very well be that your parent had been abused. Abuse breeds abuse in a cyclical nature. If you find yourself being abusive of other people, that should help you understand how your own abuse was possible. But being angry or engaging in blame over abuse you suffered or self-blame for abuse you are responsible for will only detract from your healing. Anger may have the power to cleanse, but continued anger blocks healing. Maintaining your sense of outrage and resentment toward the unfairness of life and toward those who abused you keeps you in bondage to that blaming mode. The anger ceases to cleanse and starts to control. In order for the anger to continue, you must constantly feed the fire, reliving and reexperiencing the anger and rage, thus stoking the fires of blame.

As these fires are stoked, the flame burns red hot. Tall, leaping flames of rage erupt. You are ready to devour everything in your path. You feel powerful and in control, perhaps for the first time in your life. It feels good. You feel strong—so strong that no one will ever try to hurt you again.

You can't maintain that fire without blame—blaming yourself for the abuse you have received; blaming yourself for the abuse you have given; blaming others for both. This fire of blame will consume you.

That is why it is so important for you to get out of the blame mode. You can do that by trying to understand your abuser. So often abuse occurs because of faulty parenting patterns, without malicious intent. Abuse also can happen when an adult simply forgets what it means to be a child, when a parent stops taking the time to view the world from three feet high.

Sometimes abuse occurs and it really has nothing to do with you—it just happens to you. The other person is tired, careless, stressed, distracted, moody, or any number of things. Every single one of us has felt this way and acted toward others in this way. Every single one of us is to blame for something.

Sometimes abuse occurs because the other person is weak. They know what they should do but just do not have the strength, courage, or motivation to do it. When we are in relationship with other people, we want them to be strong enough to overcome their weaknesses so they can love us as they should. If only our desire for their strength could somehow infuse them with that strength! But this rarely happens. Blame will not strengthen them into suddenly overcoming their weaknesses. Instead, blame causes them to become weaker still, further undercutting any motivation or strength they may have to change. Blame gets you nowhere but backwards.

Getting past the blame helps you get past the abuse and get on with your life. You get out of the blame mode by trying to understand what was really behind your abuse. Was the other person evil? If your abuser was truly evil, blaming him or her will have little negative effect on the abuser and a great negative effect on you. Constant blame will only allow the abuser to continue to hurt you more, because it keeps you stuck in the abuse cycle.

Was the other person not evil but weak? So much abuse is done by people who really ought to know better but for some reason can't see what it is they are doing. Both abused and abuser can be caught in the trap of ignoring and denying, accepting and perpetuating. Blame continues the cycle. Forgiveness ends it.

The Healing Power of Forgiveness

Emotional abusers seek to strip away your sense of control and security. In an obsessive need to control their surroundings, emotional abusers use inappropriate ways to ensure the compliance of those with whom they are in relationship. Their need to control is so great that they cannot tolerate anyone else retaining control over their own lives. They feel as if they have no control, so they rip yours away and take it for themselves. Forgiveness, however, returns you to a state of being in control. No one can bestow your forgiveness on another person but you. You are in total control of your own power to forgive.

Forgiveness does not mean that you forget all that has happened to you. It still hurts. But living obsessed with the pain and determined to continue the blame only perpetuates the damage. Forgiveness validates that there is something to forgive. By saying, "I forgive," you forgive the situation even if it is difficult to forgive the person, and you receive back control. Depending on your situation, you may or may not be able to forgive your abuser face-to-face. If you are the abuser, you can forgive yourself face-to-face. You can look at yourself and your situation. You can read your own heart and acknowledge your own desire to change and grow.

If your abuser is out of your life, you can attempt to contact that person through a phone call, letter, or visit. However, it is important to realize that it may not be physically possible for you to be in the same place as your abuser. If the abuser still has a powerful effect on you, any contact you have could be damaging and should be avoided until you are strong enough. It is also possible that your abuser has come to understand the damage he or she has caused and may have come to you already seeking forgiveness. If that is the case, the gift of forgiveness you give will be a blessing to you both.

If your abuser is dead, you can still forgive. The person may no longer be alive to receive your forgiveness, but you can still grant it. Sometimes it is easier to forgive the person after he or she has died. There is something about the finality of the grave that awaits us all that can help put forgiveness into perspective. Also, once the person is dead, his or her ability to cause you further damage is severely limited. The person can take no further present or future action to hurt you. Your forgiveness, however, allows you to have the final word, if you will, on the relationship. Although the abuser can no longer be affected by what you do, your forgiveness can affect you.

Remember, the most important person forgiveness is going to help is you. Forgiving allows you to go on with your life. If you are able to forgive face-to-face, you should do so, but it is not necessary to actually be with the person in order for you to forgive.

If the abuser is in denial over the abusive behavior, he or she won't accept your forgiveness. Even your granting forgiveness will most likely be met with abuse and hostility. In such cases a letter or a short, to-the-point phone call would be more appropriate than a physical confrontation.

When in doubt, start with something safe, like a letter. I would even choose a letter over email. An email message can be reacted to by a simple click of the "Reply" button. But the time and effort you take to compose a letter requires at least some time and effort to respond back. Put your forgiveness down on paper where you are able to choose your words in the safety of your own home. Depending on how your letter is received, you can determine whether to follow up with another letter, phone call, or actual visit.

There is no set way to deliver the forgiveness. Whatever the method, you must determine in your own mind that you are going to forgive. How you go about delivering that forgiveness is up to you. Your response and attitude toward your abuser is totally up to you. It is just one step in reclaiming your personal power.

Reclaiming Your Personal Power

For much of your life, you were bombarded with words, actions, and ideas that were designed to make you think you were powerless. It's time to change that. You have worth and value. You have rights and power that never should have been taken from you. You have the right not to be verbally abused. You have the power to say no if someone tries to hurt you. You have the right to get on with your life and put your past behind you. You have the power to start the process of healing.

Even by reading this book you are saying to yourself that you believe you have the power to change. The messages of your abuse can be recorded over by relearning and reclaiming your sense of self. It is high time you found out about the real you.

If you are still in an abusive relationship, it will be difficult but not impossible for you to reclaim your personal power. But doing so will be confrontational to the person who is so aggressively trying to rob you of it. You may find it necessary to remove yourself from relationship with this abusive person while you change or until he or she changes.

You need to reclaim the right to make your own decisions, even if they differ from the decisions of others. Remind yourself daily that you are an intelligent, responsible individual who has the capacity to direct the course of your own life. If you feel the need to gain wisdom and guidance in finding your true self, seek out a trusted friend or, if you are able, a professional counselor. Only choose a person you feel safe with!

Start small as you learn to use your personal power. Perhaps you might begin by reorganizing your physical space—your house or apartment. Is it really the way you want it to be? Or has someone else unduly influenced your choices? What about your wardrobe? Are those really the clothes you like to wear? Or is that message tape in your head doing your shopping for you? How about the job you're at? Is that really what you want to be doing? How about the relationship you're in? Since each individual is different, your responses will be different as well. What will be common, though, is beginning to have a say in your environment, the people who are around you, and how you are treated by those people.

Reclaiming your personal power will mean learning to say yes to yourself when needed and no to others when warranted.

Using Common Sense to Avoid Conflicts

The greatest common sense you can use is to get out of an abusive situation if you see no immediate hope of change. This does not mean you must sever the relationship completely, but it may be necessary to put it on hold for a while. Abusive people are toxic people. They poison the relationships they are in through their attitudes and actions. In order to heal, you must first detoxify yourself by limiting contact with abusive individuals.

If you must maintain a relationship with a current or former abuser, try never to meet him or her alone. If your abuser was a parent, take a friend, spouse, or sibling with you when you meet. Try meeting at a location other than the home (for example, a restaurant or store), and bring someone else with you, explaining beforehand to this person that you need him or her to act as an emotional shield for you. When no such person is available, it might be wise to avoid personal contact with your abuser.

An emotional shield is a person who can support you while you are confronting your abuser. It should be a close friend, sibling, or spouse—someone who pledges before-hand to act as a buffer between you and your abuser if you start getting into trouble. Often people are "private" abus-ers. They act differently around others than they do when they feel safe and private. Just by bringing another person with you, you may be able to diffuse some of those private patterns.

Every confrontation with an abuser will be different, but the following example may show you how you could use an emotional shield if you feel it is necessary to physically meet with your abuser.

Jill decided it was finally time to confront her father. She dreaded the thought of doing it, but he continued to criticize every decision she made, even though she was married and hadn't lived under his roof for years. She wasn't sure if he would ever change, but she wanted to let him know that she had forgiven him for the way he had treated her as a child. She wanted him to know she was no longer going to allow him to deal with her in a harsh, judgmental way. She was nervous and scared but also determined.

Jill's husband, Paul, agreed to go along even though he at first insisted it was a family issue between Jill and her father. But he too was becoming tired of his father-in-law's derisive comments about Jill. Because of the strained relationship, Paul and Jill rarely went to visit her father. When they did, Jill became a different person. She acted differently, spoke differently, even dressed differently. Jill needed Paul there to remind her father that she wasn't just his little girl anymore.

They agreed to meet at a local restaurant, one that had pri-vate booths and soft lighting. Jill knew her father would have to listen to her without yelling or risk public embarrassment. Of course, he could always walk out once he had heard what she had to say, but that was a risk she was willing to take. She just couldn't put up with his behavior any longer. Since she didn't really want to cut all ties with him, this seemed the only way to deal with the problem.

It was awkward at first when they all met at the restaurant and waited in the lobby for their table. Her father knew she wanted to talk to him about something, but neither of them wanted to bring it up with a handful of strangers rubbing elbows with them.

They spoke of trivial things—the weather, local sports teams. When the conversation drifted into how Jill and Paul's daughter was doing in school, Jill felt the old tension coming back. With great relief, she heard their name being called for a table.

"Dad," Jill began after they had ordered, "you know I'll always love you."

It was her father's turn to be uncomfortable. He shifted in his seat and glanced at Paul. "Sure, honey," he said quietly.

"But, Dad, I've come to a decision about things. I just hope you'll understand." He looked puzzled but didn't respond.

"All my life," Jill continued, "it has seemed to me that you were never happy with anything I did."

At this point he tried to interrupt, to deny what she was saying. But Jill persisted.

"Please, Dad, let me finish. My grades were never good enough in school. You didn't like the clothes I wore or the friends I made. I've always wanted you to approve of me, but every time we talk, there always seems to be something I should be doing that I haven't or something I did that I shouldn't have done. I've spent my whole life wanting you, just once, to listen to what I had to say or watch what I was doing without bringing up everything you thought was wrong. I want you to let go of me, Dad. I want you to let me be who I am without interfering or criticizing."

"Why are you saying this?" her father asked, ashen-faced and embarrassed. "If I thought you were doing wrong, it was my job as a parent to say so! What was I supposed to do? Let you go off and do something stupid and get hurt? I wouldn't be a very good parent if I let you do that!"

"But, Dad," Jill said, taking a deep breath, "you never seemed to think anything I did was right. You could always find something wrong."

"Well, did you ever think it was because something *was* wrong? You pulled some pretty crazy stunts growing up! Come to think of it, this is a pretty crazy stunt. Is this what you brought me here to tell me, that I'm a bad father?" His voice had increased to a level just below shouting. Jill's eyes were beginning to flood with tears. Paul decided now was the time to speak up.

"Look, Bob," he began. "Nobody's saying you were a bad father. All Jill is asking you to do is think about how you treated her then and how you treat her now."

"I think this is between my daughter and me!"

"She's your daughter, but she's my wife and a mother herself. This affects all of us. We're just asking that you think about the way you speak to her and treat her."

"Dad, I'm not saying you meant to be mean or cruel. All I know is how you've made me feel. I still desperately want you to approve of me, but I can't spend the rest of my life trying to get something you're never going to give!"

No one spoke for a moment while their dinner was brought to the table. Slowly, her father began again in a quieter tone. "I was always so worried," he said, "that you'd hurt yourself and that it would be my fault. That I didn't teach you well enough how to ride a bike or climb a tree. That I didn't give you the skills you needed to choose your friends or stay out of trouble. I never wanted you to get hurt. . . ."

"But I did get hurt, Daddy," Jill told him softly. "You hurt me. . . ."

Paul just let his wife and her father talk. He really didn't have to say more; he just had to be there. As Jill's father tried to understand how she saw things that had happened in the past, Paul was able to provide a few examples he had seen in the time they had been married. But mostly he just moved into the background, asserting himself only when the conversation seemed to be tilting out of balance.

There are other sorts of shielding you can use besides another person. Using the telephone is another way to buffer yourself if you need to remain in contact with an abuser. There are a variety of ways to shorten or terminate a conversation on the telephone. The lack of face-to-face contact and the physical distance between you can help you separate yourself from the conversation if necessary.

If the mere presence of this person causes you anxiety but you just don't feel you can withdraw from the relationship completely, try to carry on a long-distance relationship by mail. Often this is an excellent way to begin the process of learning more about the other person, which may allow you to feel comfortable enough to eventually confront him or her about the abusive behavior. It can also be a good test of the abuser's willingness to make necessary changes in his or her relationship with you.

Nine Steps When Someone Hurts You

Being able to put your past abuse into perspective doesn't mean you will be immune from being hurt in the present. If you are around people for very long, you will end up being hurt by someone! Your past patterns of dealing with being hurt are not those you want to continue. So here are some steps you can take to deal with current situations. They will help you to develop some new techniques and keep you from reacting to new hurts in old ways.

1. Recognize the offense for what it is. Is it intentional? Is it unintentional? Is it a misunderstanding? Listen to what your heart tells you about what happened. Usually your gut reaction is a good indicator of what you really think. However, listen to the truth behind that reaction. Your reaction may be an old one coming up from your past. As we talked about before, choose to respond intentionally instead of reacting instinctively.

   It may be helpful to write out just what was said. Often it will look different to you on paper. You may also want to write out how you felt about what happened. You can use this to determine what you are going to do about it. This will help strengthen your ability to respond and not engage in a delayed reaction. Allow someone you trust to read through what you've written and provide feedback, not so they can make your decisions for you but so they can assist you, if needed, in articulating your thoughts.

2. Resist the tendency to defend your position. If you determine that you need to confront the person who has hurt you, offer only your point of view about the incident. It is amazing how many confrontations can be diffused by removing defensiveness and hostility. When you stick to what you are feeling, you give the other person permission to explain his or her point of view. Then together you can come to a consensus, hopefully resulting in mutual forgiveness.

3. Give up the need to be right. This can be an unfortunate leftover from your past abuse and can escalate a bad situation into a worse one. Other people are entitled to their own thoughts and opinions. When differences of opinion arise, it does not necessarily dictate that one person is right and the other person is wrong. They may simply disagree.

4. Recognize and apologize for anything you may have done to contribute to the situation. Make certain, however, that it is a legitimate wrong or oversight and not false guilt brought on by past abuse. However, don't assume that past abuse gives you a pass on your own responsibility for your actions. Treating someone badly and then blaming it on something in your past does nothing to help the other person in the present, who is not to blame for your past abuse.

5. Respond versus react—learn to be proactive. This will require you to pause long enough to take the opportunity to think and evaluate. Sometimes just waiting will add needed perspective. By responding and not

just reacting, you exert control over your behavior. You're probably saying, "I know, I know," but I cannot emphasize this enough. Your past emotional abuse has caused you to develop some pretty sensitive buttons that others can inadvertently push without understanding the consequences. Learning this skill will help you respond appropriately, giving your responses greater power and meaning to others.

6. Adopt an attitude of bridge building as opposed to attacking or retreating. A conciliatory attitude is much easier for everyone to deal with than a hostile, defensive one. Practice maintaining an attitude of love and acceptance. This doesn't mean you agree with the person who has hurt you and with what he or she has done, but rather that you have chosen to respond in a certain, predetermined way. When you present your concerns with a door open to reconciliation, I think you'll find yourself pleased at how often the other person will opt to walk through.

7. Realize you may be the target of someone's anger but not the source of that anger. You may find yourself in the unenviable position of being the proverbial straw that broke someone else's back. Take responsibility only for your part. Avoid falling into the trap of accepting false guilt from others. It is not your place in life to absorb the anger of others, no matter how you've been treated in the past. Deflect what doesn't belong to you. Other people need to be responsible for their own anger and will have to learn to deal with it themselves.

8. Create your personal limits. This is part of reclaiming your personal power. You have the right to define what your limits are and to insist that they be respected.

You probably are aware of behaviors you have put up with in the past that really annoy you and have made you feel that you were being treated disrespectfully or unfairly. You have a right to let your objections be heard. It needn't be in an angry, vengeful way but rather in an assertive, positive way that says, "I respect who I am as a person, and I would like you to do the same."

9. Realize that even if someone has hurt you, that need not take away your personal happiness. Remember, you are in charge of your attitude and response. You can get over it and go on. If the hurt was unintentional, ask yourself, *Why am I magnifying it by holding on to it?* If the hurt was intentional and forgiven, ask yourself, *If the person has asked for my forgiveness and moved on, why am I still stuck in the pain?* If the hurt was intentional and unforgiven, tell yourself, *I choose to forgive the pain the person caused me so I can move past it.* Then reassert yourself and determine to be happy. It's a choice you should reserve for yourself.

Finding and Maintaining Healthy Relationships

If you want to maintain a healthy relationship, you must first find one. A healthy relationship is one in which each individual experiences positive, uplifting consequences from the relationship, in which individual opinions and personalities are respected, and in which trust is the cornerstone on which the relationship is built. If you have had trouble in the past finding someone who desired that kind of relationship, don't give up! Keep looking! For each one of you out there looking one way, someone else is looking back. Keep looking until you find each other.

When seeking a healthy relationship, be alert to signs of a possible abuser. Pay attention to how the other person speaks to you and about you. Make certain you avoid people who show signs of any of the abusive behaviors we've discussed.

Take your time and don't rush. If you have been looking for a relationship for a while, you may be tempted to dive right in once you find one. However, it would be prudent for you to take it slow. Find ways to be with the person in a variety of situations. Meet this person's friends and family. Observe how this person treats friends and family, how he or she is treated by them, and how he or she treats you. What you see in one relationship can give clues to the truth in all different relationships.

As you are looking at the other person, don't forget to keep an eye on yourself. Be aware of how you may be affected by your abuse and how it may cause heightened patterns of perfectionism and hypersensitivity in you. Not only must you find a person with whom you want a relationship, but he or she must be able to maintain a relationship with you.

The most effective way of maintaining a healthy relationship is by becoming healthy yourself. Even though the process is painful, don't substitute working on a healthy relationship for your own self-healing. It may be that your relationship with yourself is the primary one you need to spend time and energy on first, before you work on a relationship with another person. Healthy people tend to attract healthy people. You may want to delay looking until you're farther down the road on the way to recovery yourself. If that's the case, don't begrudge the time. Take the time and effort to know yourself. I promise you won't regret it!

Look around you at friends and acquaintances who have loving relationships. You will be able to tell by the things they say and the way they act around each other whether or not it is the type of relationship you want to model. When you feel comfortable, ask questions. Gain insight from them as they talk about how they met and why they are still together. Some of the wisest counsel you can receive is from couples who have been together for many years. If your family pattern makes looking to family members such as grandparents suspect, seek out others in church, service groups, or social clubs.

Many fine books are available that deal with how to grow a healthy relationship. Take the time to read and reflect on the type of person you want to be individually and as part of a couple.

Most important, put what you learn into practice. Do not demand perfection, but keep on trying. This is part of learning to live differently than you have in the past. Once you have turned the corner away from abuse, just keep on going. Choosing to act differently can help keep you from turning back.

Up to now I have spoken about intimate relationships between couples, but many of these same rules apply for establishing and maintaining good friendships. Any time you open yourself to another person for a relationship, make sure you choose a person with whom you can feel safe and comfortable.

Traits of a Healthy Communicator

Since so much of emotional abuse is verbal and involved with how one person communicates with another, it is important to learn healthy communication in order to maintain a healthy relationship. As you communicate with those around you, remember these twelve guidelines:

1. Approach others with an attitude of gentleness and openness. Be aware of any patterns of cynicism, sarcasm, undue deference, or telling people what they want to hear. Commit to living within the moment and taking people at face value. Leave anger and hostility behind.

2. If you are attempting to solve a problem, avoid assuming a position of rightness before you even start. Your rightness implies that all others are wrong. This could lead to a defensive attitude on their part. Be open to the possibility that the problem stems from a difference of opinion. You may both be right, from each perspective. The objective is not to determine who is right and who is wrong but to find a solution to the problem together.

3. Don't be afraid to speak the truth. Speak it confidently but without a desire to harm the other person. Truth should be offered as a way to heal and help people find their way. Truth should never be used as a bludgeon against other people. When truth is used to injure another, it loses its virtue, and so does the person wielding it.

4. Work on being able to separate how you feel about what you are saying from the message you are giving. It is important not to deny your emotions, but if you allow them free rein while you are communicating, your emotions can overshadow the message itself. Intense emotions can overwhelm another person and make it virtually impossible to get your point across. Do you remember that old adage that says if you want to be noticed, whisper? In most circumstances, intense

emotions are best "whispered" in conversations instead of screamed at the top of your lungs. There are times and places for full-bore venting, but conversations with others generally are neither.

5. Be aware of the different ways men and women process information. Men and women often have differing worldviews—they may notice different details, or they may have different priority systems. This is not to be used as an excuse for unacceptable behavior, but it can help you to understand another person's perspective. Resist the temptation to consider one gender superior to another because of these style differences or because of your personal comfort level. Instead of concentrating on gender, seek instead to focus on the substance behind the style. And ask questions. If you don't understand what is being said, politely ask for clarification. You shouldn't be expected to understand everything you're told the first time.

6. Allow the other person to hold an opinion that is different from yours. Two opinions does not automatically mean a right and a wrong. If you doubt this is true, I encourage you to read through several chapters in the book of Romans, beginning with chapter 14. If God can consider such differences of opinion acceptable, we ought to be able to ourselves.

7. Attempt to communicate an attitude of acceptance and love. The healthier you become emotionally, the easier this will become. Nonetheless, work at establishing an accepting and loving demeanor as you communicate with others. Take control of your part of the conversation.

8. Make sure that your motivation to engage in the conversation is one of enhancing and improving the relationship as opposed to hurting the other person. As humans, all of us are subject to hurtful behavior and speech. Being the victim of emotional abuse does not excuse a person from speaking and acting badly toward others. All of us must be alert to how our speech and actions affect other people.

9. Allow the other person to make his or her own decisions. This goes back to the concept of control. People need the freedom to make their own decisions, even if you don't agree. They do not have the right to be hurtful, but they do have the right to choose a different path.

10. Seek to inspire trust by extending understanding to the other person and by responding honestly to what is said. Note this doesn't say "by extending agreement." You will not always agree with the other person, but you should always seek to understand him or her. Relationships are strengthened by each person's permission to speak truthfully from the heart.

11. Always make sure to seek forgiveness yourself when you make a mistake. Being able to admit your own failures will help the other person feel comfortable enough to admit his or her failures. Seek to be transparent in your relationships. This means acknowledging your own faults and allowing other people to feel safe to acknowledge theirs. When we trust each other with who we really are, we encourage intimacy.

12. Be accountable for what you say you will do. I cannot emphasize this last point enough. This means living honestly with yourself and others. In the past,

emotional abuse may have robbed you of relationships based on truth and integrity, but you can intentionally choose to live out a different pattern in your life today.

Maintaining communication within your relationships will require work, but the rewards will far outweigh your efforts.

Discovering Your Gifts and Talents

You are unique. No one else is made quite like you. Each of us has a variety of talents and, I believe, at least one true gift. Finding what your gifts and talents are can enhance your sense of self-worth. Practicing those gifts and talents will automatically add to your self-esteem.

A gift is usually defined as some activity you are exceptional at that requires no work on your part. You simply are able to do whatever it is with very little effort. It can be anything from speaking in public to having a green thumb in the garden. Generally it is a thing that gives you great joy, and when you engage in it, you feel confident of yourself and what you are doing.

A talent, on the other hand, is something you are good at that requires practice. If you don't practice your talents, you tend to lose them. Often people choose one of their talents to use as their career. Doctors have a talent for medicine; accountants have a talent with numbers; bakers have a talent in the kitchen. Each has trained in his or her field and continues to practice and hone his or her skills.

The negative messages from emotional abuse may have robbed you of the knowledge that you are special—that you are gifted and talented. By discovering your gifts and talents, you expose those messages for the lies they are.

If you are unsure of what your gifts and talents are, try remembering what you enjoyed doing as a child before other people stepped in to tell you what you were good at. Take a class at a community center or local college. Don't be afraid to take risks and try different things. There is no need to attain perfection in your gifts and talents; just find out what they are. Your gifts and talents should add to your quality of life and improve your sense of self-worth.

Ask God to show you your talents and gifts. While you may have some idea of what you're talented in, your gifts may catch you by surprise. If you have the opportunity, you may want to take a spiritual gifts survey, either on your own or through your faith community.

If you're not sure what your talents are or how you have been gifted by God, don't just sit at home doing nothing. Get out and get busy. Find some good work to do, and do it. I've heard it said that it is not our ability that God desires but our availability. If you make yourself available for service, you may very well find your talents and gifts along the way.

Characteristics of a Healthy Problem Solver

Within any relationship you have, the time will come when a problem or conflict arises. Your past model of how to deal with that conflict will be faulty because of your abuse. Try these fifteen steps to work your way through to a solution:

1. Seek to resolve and deal successfully with the problem and not just be declared the winner.

2. Face your conflict instead of avoiding it.

3. Understand that different people can have different points of view concerning the problem and the best way to solve it.

4. Be clear about what is and is not acceptable in solving the problem. Do not accept abusive behavior of any kind.

5. Remember that people do make mistakes and have a need for forgiveness.

6. Take the initiative and forgive first.

7. Avoid the temptation to exact vengeance for any hurt inflicted.

8. Realize that there are times when the world is unfair and that sometimes you will be treated unfairly by others.

9. Approach the solution to the problem in a whole-person way: intellectually, emotionally, spiritually, and relationally.

10. Attempt to solve only one problem at a time. One is generally enough!

11. Anticipate a positive outcome to your problem solving.

12. Be consistent in your effort to come to a resolution without trying to force a predetermined solution.

13. Understand the power you have to provide a solution through an understanding of who you are.

14. Search for commonsense solutions.

15. Be aware of verbal and nonverbal communication.

Healthy problem solvers are better able to maintain supportive relationships through increased communication. Skill and improvement in this area can be used to improve other areas. Give yourself permission to grow in life skills.

Under ideal circumstances, you would have learned how to navigate healthy problem solving as you matured. Instead, you learned a dysfunctional pattern through the emotional abuse you suffered. Give yourself time to integrate these skills into your life.

As an exercise, take the list of fifteen characteristics above and reorder them according to your priorities. What struck you as being the most important in your own life today? Commit to using that as a starting place. Next, write down the characteristic you want to work on and place it somewhere you can see it daily. Remind yourself of your commitment to integrating this trait into your own character. As it becomes more normal to you, write down the next one on your list, and so on. Allow these characteristics to permeate your life and relationships.

How to Recognize Progress

Finally, it is important for you to understand that getting over emotional abuse and living for the future is not a one-time revelation; it is a healing *process*. Just as injuries and illnesses are seldom healed overnight, your emotional injuries will need time to heal.

This isn't a race you are trying to win. Avoid the perfectionist reaction of wanting to fix everything in as little time as possible—to show everyone and yourself how fast you can get over your abuse.

The most any of us can ask for as we go through life is to grow toward being better people. Not perfect people, but better people—better toward ourselves, better toward our families, better toward the people we come into contact with each day. Doing so will not only bring about a more pleasant response from the people we meet, but it will also help us to feel good about ourselves.

Emotional abuse has been responsible for you feeling bad about yourself for too long. Now it's time to start feeling good! Now it's time to start knowing the wonderful person you really are!

It was ten o'clock in the morning, and Meg sat in her bathrobe drinking coffee. As she pulled deeply at her cigarette, she looked around and realized she hated everything about her life.

Her cluttered apartment. The stacks of unwashed dishes in the sink and on the counter with food drying to hardness.

Her job. The mindless, numbing repetition of inputting orders for hardware nails into an impersonal electronic box.

Her relationships. A boyfriend who never seemed to come home unless he was too drunk to be of much good. A mother she couldn't stand who kept calling on the phone to remind her of what a mess she had made of her life.

Her looks. Thirty pounds overweight. Lines and wrinkles that seemed to appear overnight.

Meg was only twenty-seven years old, but she felt like fifty. Worse—she felt like her mother at fifty.

It seemed that somewhere along the line something had gone terribly wrong. This wasn't the life she thought she would have. She remembered reading a beautiful book when she was four years old. It had big, bright pages with pictures of a sunny little house with happy, smiling people on a long, tree-lined street. Oh, how she had loved that book.

She had asked her daddy to read it over and over again. She had memorized the pictures and would sit and dream about the kind of house she would have when she grew up.

Twenty-three years later, the book was long gone. And so was the dream. Her father had left the family after the birth of her brother when she was eight years old. He had found someone he liked better than her mother. The last fight her parents had, her father had yelled at her mother so loudly that she could still hear him screaming, "I just don't need you anymore!"

At age eight Meg had been certain her dad was talking about her. At twenty-seven she wasn't so sure anymore, but she still hadn't spoken to him in years.

After Meg's father left the family, times were hard, and her mother had to get a different job to support the family. Her mother was always tired at night, and Meg ended up taking on many of the household chores her mother didn't have the energy to do. Her younger brother, Rob, never seemed to have to do as much as she did. He was the baby of the family, and Meg always knew her mother loved him more.

As soon as she could, Meg spent more and more time away from the house. She had been pretty in high school, but that was before drinking too much had aged her body and clouds of cigarette smoke had yellowed her skin, hands, and teeth. Now she felt invisible. No one looked at her with interest. Her current boyfriend only seemed to be interested in the money she brought home. Yes, back in high school she had really been something to look at, with boys eager to be seen with her. But she always seemed to choose the hard-luck cases—the ones with problems at school or at home. She figured they were just like her.

Instead of going to college, Meg had gone to work right out of high school to help with the family bills. Her mother had developed a chronic back condition and was only drawing disability benefits. Meg had wanted to take up writing, but she ended up as a checker at the local mini-mart.

After seven years of standing on her feet all day, Meg had gotten the data-entry job. At least now she could sit down. Of course, that's when the thirty pounds had come on.

Over the years Meg had several relationships—only one serious. She had wanted to get married, but he said he didn't want to be that tied down. Six months after she had started pressing him on it, he left. The boyfriend she had now was a drunk, but at least he wouldn't leave her. His unemployment would run out soon, and where else was he going to get his beer money?

What ever happened to the bright, sunny house with the happy, smiling people on that long, tree-lined street? How in the world had that picture ever turned into the one Meg saw as she looked around? She sat the rest of the morning and all afternoon at the kitchen table, smoking, unable to move more than a few feet to the sink or the bathroom.

Come on, Meg! she said to herself as evening approached. *There has to be more to life than this! That house is out there! There has to be a way to find it!*

Sitting there, Meg realized that if she hadn't found that house by now, she probably wasn't going to be able to on her own. She would need some help. Getting out the phone book, she started flipping through the pages. She had almost shut the book when she saw the word *Therapists* at the top of a page. In the back of her mind she could hear what her mother would have to say about that. But she ignored her mother's voice and searched until she found an ad she liked.

"A place of hope," she read. Hope. That was what she needed.

"Why are you here?" I asked Meg on her first visit.

"I want you to help me find this house," she said, and smiled. I looked puzzled, and she proceeded to tell me what I have just told you.

Inside the house were all of those special things she had dreamed of and wanted as a child that somehow never seemed to happen. Inside the house was a father who loved her, a mother who wasn't too busy, a brother who was more than a threat to her place in the family. Inside the house was who she wanted to be, with a family of her own.

Together we began to look for the house. We started from the house she grew up in and then moved through all the houses she had lived in since then and on to the one she was living in now. We talked about what happened in those houses with the people who lived inside them. We talked about why she so desperately wanted the sunny house.

Over the course of our time together, Meg began to feel stronger, to feel better about herself. She decided it wasn't good for her body to drink so much. Even though it was hard to face each day without it, about three months into her search, she entered into treatment to stop drinking. The cigarettes took a little bit longer, but eventually she was able to cut back dramatically in the number she smoked each day and then to quit entirely. For several months, though, she would sit in my office with an unlit cigarette in her hand.

Meg still hadn't found the house, but she decided until she did that she could do a better job of taking care of the one she had. Wanting to utilize her knack for typing, she posted fliers at the local college advertising that she typed term papers for money. With that money she hired a house cleaner to come in and help her get a handle on her surroundings. Coming home to a clean house made her feel wonderful, especially since she didn't have to do it all herself. And she found it was easier to keep clean if it started out that way in the first place.

Typing term papers had rekindled Meg's love of writing. She made suggestions on several papers and was surprised when they were well received. One day when she was at the college putting up more fliers, she decided to sign up for a writing class herself. She decided that maybe she would take enough classes to get another job for which she could use her writing more. Although she did data entry at work, she knew now that it was only a temporary job while she continued her schooling. Knowing that seemed to make the days go better. Her attitude at work improved, and co-workers began to notice, taking the opportunity to approach her more often.

When she had given up smoking, Meg had gained several pounds and was having a hard time getting them off. With all the other progress she was experiencing, she didn't want to make a big deal about the weight, but clearly it bothered her. She seemed anxious to lose it but wasn't having the kind of results she had hoped for. Together we looked at her nutritional patterns and at rebalancing her body after years of unhealthy eating habits. Meg decided that instead of trying to be thin, she would concentrate on becoming healthy.

As her body and spirit were beginning to heal, Meg's physical presentation changed. The clothes she wore into my office became brighter and more fashionable. She got her hair cut and began to take some care with her appearance.

Soon she began to look more her age. Her skin and eyes became brighter. She smiled with more regularity. She actually looked alive!

Meg's boyfriend left her when she stopped drinking and supplying him with money. He started to tear up some of her things as he was leaving, and Meg had to call the police. As they were leading him off, he yelled at her in anger, "I don't need you to tell me what to do!" Hearing that he didn't need her brought up old memories and feelings of despair. It set Meg back for a while, but it forced her to realize she had been focusing a lot of her attention on the externals. It took some time for her to understand that she was strong enough to deal with the inside.

Meg took a look at her issues of abandonment by her father. She started to deal with the effects of the emotional neglect and favoritism from her mother. Calling and talking with her brother, Rob, she was able to explain to him why she had always treated him so badly growing up. She told him about the resentment she felt at how her mother seemed to like him more than her. Admitting her anger over her belief that his birth had been responsible for their father leaving was very hard. They were able to talk about things that had happened to them both as children that they had never even acknowledged before. Rob could remember details Meg didn't remember, giving a perspective to their life she hadn't seen before.

Rob was also able to supply Meg with an address and phone number for their father. Meg hadn't known it, but Rob had been keeping in contact with him for several years. Feeling a deep need to be reunited with his father, Rob had sought him out. He hadn't told Meg—afraid she would think he was taking sides against their mother. Meg wasn't sure she felt as strong as Rob, but she conceded that maybe she would write her father a letter just to see what he would say.

Her mother, on the other hand, all of a sudden had little to say. Although she was genuinely pleased that Meg was doing so well, she was reluctant to talk about the pain she had caused Meg in the past. Whenever Meg tried to find a way to talk about her feelings, her mother would clam up, not wanting to hear. Meg realized she couldn't wait for her mother to admit to what she had done, so Meg began to work on forgiving her anyway.

We had been together for over a year when one day I asked Meg what had happened to the house. She hadn't mentioned it in months.

She thought for a moment and said, "I'm the house. I don't have to go on looking for it, because it was right here all the time." She patted her chest with her hand. "And I'm putting in it all the things I've always wanted. I've never felt better about myself than I do now. I didn't used to think I deserved very much from life, so I chose to put all the good things I wanted into someplace else. Now I know they can be right here inside of me."

This book began with a story about David, the teenager who killed himself because of the despair of his abuse. David gave up hope.

Meg didn't. Through the years of her abuse, Meg kept trying. Kept living. Meg was able to come full circle.

Now it's your turn. There is hope.

13

A Time to Heal

Restoring Your Self

An understanding of who you truly are comes from the one who created you in the first place.

Emotional abuse steals away your identity. It sucks up all of the wonderful, positive characteristics of your true nature and seeks to replace them with false truths and negative images. It attempts to hijack your personal power and sense of self for the benefit and control of your abuser. It's wrong. Even if no physical abuse takes place, it's wrong. Even if no sexual coercion takes place, it's wrong. It may have taken society a while to appreciate and speak out against how wrong emotional abuse is, but God has always known.

As your creator, God knows who you are. God loves you for who you are, even if you were not loved by others in the past and even if you have difficulty loving yourself now. While others were abusing your fragile sense of self, your secret self has always been safe with God. There has not been a moment when you have been hidden from him. Listen to King David speaking about God's steadfast connection to those he loves, in Psalm 139:1–18:

> O LORD, you have searched me
>   and you know me.
> You know when I sit and when I rise;
>   you perceive my thoughts from afar.
> You discern my going out and my lying down;
>   you are familiar with all my ways.
> Before a word is on my tongue,
>   you know it completely, O LORD.
>
> You hem me in—behind and before;
>   you have laid your hand upon me.
> Such knowledge is too wonderful for me,
>   too lofty for me to attain.
>
> Where can I go from your Spirit?
>   Where can I flee from your presence?
> If I go up to the heavens, you are there;
>   if I make my bed in the depths, you are there.
> If I rise on the wings of the dawn,
>   if I settle on the far side of the sea,
> even there your hand will guide me,
>   your right hand will hold me fast.
>
> If I say, "Surely the darkness will hide me
>   and the light become night around me,"
> even the darkness will not be dark to you;
>   the night will shine like the day,
>   for darkness is as light to you.
>
> For you created my inmost being;
>   you knit me together in my mother's womb.

I praise you because I am fearfully and wonderfully made;
your works are wonderful,
I know that full well.
My frame was not hidden from you
when I was made in the secret place.
When I was woven together in the depths of the
earth,
your eyes saw my unformed body.
All the days ordained for me
were written in your book
before one of them came to be.

How precious to me are your thoughts, O God!
How vast is the sum of them!
Were I to count them,
they would outnumber the grains of sand.
When I awake,
I am still with you.

God's Steadfast Presence

Realizing the nature of your emotional abuse can seem like
wakening after a long and terrible nightmare. The images are
in the past, but the effects are still very much in the present.
At a time such as this, it is imperative to realize that God is
still with you. In fact, he has never left you.

In the course of counseling those with emotional abuse,
a time comes when they stop denying or excusing or avoiding the truth of the abuse. The ramifications of how this has
affected their lives hit home, unfiltered. If they are Christians,
often they will ask, in essence, "Where was God when I was

being abused?" The answer is found in Psalm 139—even in the midst of the abuse, God was there to guide them and hold them fast. In the darkness of the abuse, God was able to see them clearly for who they truly were, not the person their abusers were trying to make them out to be.

Who You Are Is Safe in Him

To allow God to reintroduce you to the person you really are, you must make a commitment to resist thinking of yourself in the murky, damaged light of your abuse. For truly, whenever your abuser tried to make you perceive yourself a certain way, your abuser was really revealing his or her own nature. All of the negative things your abuser attempted to make you believe of yourself were most probably true of your abuser. His or her projection has cast a shadow on your true image, which is a bright and beautiful creation of God.

God has kept that shining core of yourself safe for all this time. Your restoration has always been his plan. It doesn't matter how far your abuse has taken you, it is always possible for God to find you and bring you back to yourself. There is nowhere you can go that he cannot find you. For your abuser, these words have ominous implications. For you, they are words of hope.

Using God's Filter

God created you as a beautiful and special child of his. It was always his plan for your relationships to polish and brighten this image. The relationships God has established are meant to enhance life, not damage it. Through the sin of others with whom you have had emotionally abusive relationships, your image has been tarnished and clouded. It's time to change that.

You are wonderful—God says so! Therefore, it's time to evaluate your relationships through God's filter and seek to strengthen and maintain those that agree with God that you are "fearfully and wonderfully made." If you have suffered under a past relationship that was emotionally abusive, the lie of that relationship can be replaced with the truth of your worth in God. If you are currently in an emotionally abusive relationship, the lie of that relationship needs to be exposed to the truth of your worth in God. To avoid an emotionally abusive relationship in the future, you need to carry the truth of your worth in God with you wherever you go.

A time may come when you realize that you must withdraw from a certain relationship if the other person refuses to treat you with the respect and love that God intends for all of your relationships. Withdrawing from the relationship does not necessarily mean ending it. Rather, disconnecting from the other person gives that person the opportunity to do some searching of his or her own. This could be a relationship with a friend, spouse, parent, or child. Hopefully your abuser will use this time to come to a better understanding of who God knows you to be, who God wants him or her to be, and who God wants him or her to be with you. If so, you will be blessed separately and collectively. If not, God is still able to bless you in your desire to be made whole again in him.

Filling in the Gaps

If it is necessary for you to withdraw from relationships, don't panic. Concentrate instead on strengthening your relationship with God. Whether or not you are able to reestablish and redefine the abusive relationship, the time you spend with God will not be wasted. We enter this world with God as our companion, and each of us will leave this world alone, except for him. While it is God's desire to bless us with connections and relationships when here, these relationships were never meant to circumvent or replace our love for and connection to him.

Initially, those who are working on a restoration of their sense of self should be cautious when entering into new relationships, especially romantic relationships. First should come healing from past relationships before you rush headlong into a new one. You need to allow yourself time to heal and time for God to restore you. When healing and restoration have had a chance to work in your life, then it will be time to look for other people with whom to enter into healthy relationships. One of the patterns I have seen in those who have been emotionally abused is jumping from one relationship to the next without time for reflection and personal growth in between. It's okay to wait awhile after leaving an emotionally abusive relationship. With God as your core relationship, you will know when and be prepared to enter into future relationships.

Step by Step, Day by Day

As you reconnect with your true self and with God, expect the process to take time. You are shedding the old persona, based on the abuse you have suffered, and are replacing it with a new understanding of who you are in God. This is a significant task and one that, quite simply, will take time. But the amazing thing about God is that he doesn't wait for the end of the journey to bless you. Rather, his presence and his love will be with you all along the way. So commit to walking with him as your guide, step by step, day by day.

How do you do this?

Work on your relationship with God each day through prayer. Talk to him. Get to know his voice and his answers to your questions. Communicate with God. When you are in a relationship with another person, you work on that relationship through talking together. It is no different with God.

Experience God through his Word. Some people are considered to be an "open book." With God, that open book is the Bible. Come to understand your relationship with him through what he has caused to be written. You can trust what he says—he has put it in writing.

Connect with God's Spirit. God is not a three-letter word confined to a page. He is a dynamic, encompassing, divine Spirit who makes it a priority to interact with those who seek him. God's Spirit is the ultimate soul mate for every person. This connection is intimate and revealing, but don't be frightened of it. Remember, God already knows everything there is to know about you. In fact, he knows you better than you know yourself. You can relax in his love and be yourself.

Continue to learn. At the back of this book, you will find a resource list of other books you can read to help further your recovery. Each recommendation comes with a short paragraph to let you know a little bit about the book and how it might be helpful to you. Check out any that strike a chord.

Allow God to continue to speak to you through other books as he has with this one.

Finding Time

You probably don't have time to go off and work exclusively on your relationship with yourself and with God. And most likely you are in a variety of relationships. You may still have a relationship with the person who has a pattern of emotionally abusing you. Whatever your other relationships, you must protect this time to grow with God, because it is vital for your recovery and healing. During each day, carve out time for yourself. Be creative if necessary. Pray while driving to pick up the kids at school. Read your Bible during a break at work. Meditate on God's Spirit while taking a walk through your neighborhood. Get up in the morning a few minutes early to have some alone time with God. Find a weekday or evening Bible study in the community to attend. God will not allow whatever time you are able to sincerely give him to be unproductive. This is the Creator who made the universe out of nothing—trust him to make good use of your time together!

Fresh Eyes

If you grew up in a religious household where emotional abuse took place, you may need to view God with fresh eyes. This is especially true if your understanding of God came from the person who emotionally abused you. That person is not trustworthy to present God to you. You will need to start fresh with God and see him with new eyes.

Please don't feel like this means you have to backtrack on spiritual understanding and start back at square one. You must trust that God has been able to reveal information about himself to you, even given the flawed delivery system known as people. Rather, view this as an exciting time of discovery and revelation. You are coming to God on your own terms, as your own person, ready to establish your own unique relationship with him. This isn't backsliding; it's called spiritual growth!

My prayer is that you will continue to heal from the scars of emotional abuse.

May you become a strong, resilient person who, through your experiences, develops an extra measure of compassion and empathy for the tremendous amount of pain in this world.

May you come to know yourself as God knows you, and to follow his love to greater love for yourself and others.

May you hold hope close to your heart as a promise and a gift from God.

Emotional Abuse Checklist

Answer "Agree," "Disagree," or "Unsure" to the following questions. When a blank line appears, fill in the blank with the most appropriate person or relationship, and then answer the question.

Agree	Disagree	Unsure

1. I feel I have been emotionally abused in the past.

☐   ☐   ☐

2. I never felt like my father approved of me.

☐   ☐   ☐

3. I had a hard time pleasing my mother when I was growing up.

☐   ☐   ☐

4. I would often find ways to avoid going home.

☐   ☐   ☐

Agree	Disagree	Unsure

5. Growing up, I felt disconnected from my parents or those taking care of me.

☐ ☐ ☐

6. I rarely felt safe at home as a child.

☐ ☐ ☐

7. Everyone always wanted me to be more than I was.

☐ ☐ ☐

8. I wasn't allowed to express my emotions as a child.

☐ ☐ ☐

9. Others in the family picked on me growing up

☐ ☐ ☐

10. When I think back on my childhood, more bad memories come to mind than good memories.

☐ ☐ ☐

11. I was constantly lectured to as a child.

☐ ☐ ☐

12. Growing up, I was always wrong and my _____ was always right.

☐ ☐ ☐

13. I never felt that my reasons why I did or thought something were taken into account.

☐ ☐ ☐

14. My _____ had a way of always letting me know how stupid I was.

☐ ☐ ☐

	Agree	Disagree	Unsure

15. I'd often get into a shouting match with _____, but I never felt I won.

☐   ☐   ☐

16. I seemed to be the butt of all of the jokes in my family.

☐   ☐   ☐

17. My _____ always reminded me of how bad I was.

☐   ☐   ☐

18. Whenever I got into a fight with _____, he/she would always bring up everything bad I'd ever done. It seemed like I wasn't just fighting that battle but refighting every battle that had gone on before.

☐   ☐   ☐

19. Sometimes I felt like running into my room and putting a pillow over my head so I didn't have to listen anymore.

☐   ☐   ☐

20. My house was rarely peaceful and quiet when I was growing up.

☐   ☐   ☐

21. I kept trying to please, but nothing seemed to work.

☐   ☐   ☐

22. Often my _____ yelled at me instead of speaking to me.

☐   ☐   ☐

	Agree	Disagree	Unsure

23. I wasn't allowed to question _____'s decisions growing up.

☐   ☐   ☐

24. My _____ never actually hit me, but the threat was always implied.

☐   ☐   ☐

25. My _____'s moods were always up and down. I could never be sure from moment to moment what the mood would be.

☐   ☐   ☐

26. Growing up I had two families. The private one was kept secret from what we showed in public.

☐   ☐   ☐

27. I didn't feel like the favorite child in the family.

☐   ☐   ☐

28. When I was growing up, my father told me things about my mother that were embarrassing. I felt more like a spouse than a child.

☐   ☐   ☐

29. Sometimes I felt more like my _____'s "buddy" than his/her child.

☐   ☐   ☐

30. When I was a child, God was presented to me as a vengeful "superparent" who would punish me for the evil inside me.

☐   ☐   ☐

Agree	Disagree	Unsure

31. My father never seemed to want to spend any time with me.

☐ ☐ ☐

32. I was often left alone as a child.

☐ ☐ ☐

33. My _____ seemed happier when I didn't bother him/her.

☐ ☐ ☐

34. I often felt like the parent instead of the child.

☐ ☐ ☐

35. When I finally was able to leave the house, I felt free.

☐ ☐ ☐

36. I dreaded birthdays and special events because I'd hope my _____ would show up and he/she wouldn't.

☐ ☐ ☐

37. Most of the time I felt on my own.

☐ ☐ ☐

38. I often felt my _____ would be better off without having to take care of me.

☐ ☐ ☐

39. I tried to earn affection by doing everything right.

☐ ☐ ☐

40. I often felt it was my fault my _____ left.

☐ ☐ ☐

Agree	Disagree	Unsure

41. I don't feel people know the "real" me.

    ☐ ☐ ☐

42. I often automatically take the blame if something goes wrong.

    ☐ ☐ ☐

43. I don't speak up for myself when I'm confronted by someone else.

    ☐ ☐ ☐

44. I don't trust my own judgment and will go to others to make decisions.

    ☐ ☐ ☐

45. I will go with someone else's opinion, even if it goes against my gut feeling.

    ☐ ☐ ☐

46. My current relationship could be called an abusive one.

    ☐ ☐ ☐

47. Even though I'm abused, I feel I love my mate.

    ☐ ☐ ☐

48. I really believe my mate will change.

    ☐ ☐ ☐

49. I feel like I have to conceal part of me from my mate.

    ☐ ☐ ☐

50. It's hard for me to trust and be intimate with another person.

    ☐ ☐ ☐

	Agree	Disagree	Unsure

51. I use alcohol/drugs to help get through life.
    ☐   ☐   ☐

52. My mate treats me worse after using alcohol/drugs.
    ☐   ☐   ☐

53. During times of stress, I sometimes have trouble breathing.
    ☐   ☐   ☐

54. Sometimes I just feel too tired to cope with life.
    ☐   ☐   ☐

55. I experience a lot of digestive problems.
    ☐   ☐   ☐

56. I am a bulimic, an anorexic, or a compulsive overeater.
    ☐   ☐   ☐

57. Often I'm anxious for no discernible reason.
    ☐   ☐   ☐

58. Doctors can't seem to find out what's wrong with me even though I go in with specific complaints.
    ☐   ☐   ☐

59. I am often incapacitated by migraine headaches.
    ☐   ☐   ☐

60. I have experienced brief, intense moments of sheer panic when I'm sure I'm having a heart attack.
    ☐   ☐   ☐

61. I have an abnormal fear of normal things.
    ☐   ☐   ☐

How to Use This Questionnaire

Go back over this questionnaire and note those questions you said you agreed with. Take a second look at any you answered "Unsure" and try to pinpoint whether you agree or disagree. If you are still unsure, that's all right, but often saying you are unsure is a way to avoid having to accept the answer.

Questions 1–10 will help you identify the feelings you had as a child growing up. As you go through these questions, write down how you are feeling as you answer.

Questions 11–40 will help you identify the different types of emotional abuse you have experienced. Remember, emotional abuse can take different forms, and you may have experienced a variety of abuse. Questions 11–20 deal with verbal abuse. Questions 21–30 cover emotional abuse conveyed through the actions of others. Questions 31–40 look at emotional abuse conveyed through the neglect of others.

Finally, questions 41–61 deal with the repercussions of emotional abuse through relational effects and physical effects.

Again, here is the breakdown of these questions:

Questions 1–10: Identifying past patterns and feelings

Questions 11–20: Pinpointing verbally abusive behavior

Questions 21–30: Pinpointing emotional abuse through actions

Questions 31–40: Highlighting emotional abuse through emotional and physical neglect

Questions 41–50: Personal and relational effects

Questions 51–61: Physical effects

Once you have gone through this list, think over the following questions:

Do I believe recovery is possible?
Am I willing to let go of my past and live for the future?
Am I ready to forgive and move on?
Am I ready to believe in myself and in my power to change?

This book is written to support you in your quest to find healing from the scars of your emotional abuse. Some people, however, will require professional assistance to effect the type of change necessary to overcome the effects of emotional abuse. If this seems like more than you are able to do on your own, please contact Dr. Jantz and The Center for Counseling and Health Resources, Inc. Our intensive outpatient program may be the supportive environment you need to take a giant leap forward in putting your abuse behind you and reclaiming hope for the future. Our toll-free number is (888) 771-5166. For more information about our intensive treatment program for healing from emotional abuse, you can also access our website at www .aplaceofhope.com.

Notes

Chapter 5: Emotional Abuse through Actions

1. Go online to www.aplaceofhope.com to take the free anger test.

Chapter 6: Emotional Abuse through Neglect

1. Bruce D. Perry, MD, PhD, "Bonding and Attachment in Maltreated Children: Consequences of Emotional Neglect in Childhood," http://teacher.scholastic.com/professional/bruceperry/bonding.htm (accessed 28 September 2002).

Chapter 8: The Effects on Sense of Self

1. If you have suffered emotional abuse, it may be difficult for you to understand that your self-esteem is low. You have become accustomed to how you think of yourself and may not realize this represents low self-esteem. If you think this may be the case, please go online and take the depression survey found at www.aplaceofhope.com. This quiz will provide insights into how you truly think of yourself.

2. For a more in-depth discussion of inappropriate sexuality, please see Dr. Gregg Jantz with Ann McMurray, *Too Close to the Flame: Recognizing and Avoiding Sexualized Relationships* (West Monroe, LA: Howard, 1999).

Chapter 9: The Physical Effects

1. Duncan B. Clark, "How 'Negative Emotionality' Can Make You Feel Sick," Pittsburgh Adolescent Research Center, September 16, 2001, http://www.eurekalert.org/pub_releases/2001-09/ace-he091001.php (accessed 28 September 2002).

2. For a thorough discussion of the effects of depression, see Gregory L. Jantz with Ann McMurray, *Moving Beyond Depression: A Whole-Person Approach to Healing* (Colorado Springs: Shaw, 2003).

3. See Gregory L. Jantz with Ann McMurray, *Hope, Help, and Healing for Eating Disorders: A New Approach to Treating Anorexia, Bulimia, and Overeating* (Colorado Springs: Shaw, 2002).

4. John E. Sarno, MD, *Mind over Back Pain* (New York: William Marrow, 1984).

Chapter 11: Recognizing Your Abuse and Its Effects

1. The resource list at the back of this book includes other books that can aid you in your search for deeper sexual intimacy.

Resource List

The following resources are provided to assist you on your healing journey. I have found each to have valuable information on emotional abuse. The one book I place above all others is the Bible. Through it, God clearly demonstrates the love he has for you and his affirmation of your value and worth as an individual. May he provide you further insight as you seek greater understanding of yourself and of him.

Books

Benvenga, Nancy. *Healing the Wounds of Emotional Abuse: The Journey Worth the Risk* (Resurrection Press, 1996). This helpful book approaches recovery from emotional abuse from a spiritual point of view and encourages personal awareness as a child of abuse and as a parent.

Cloud, Dr. Henry, and Dr. John Townsend. *Boundaries* (Zondervan, 1992). This book is an excellent presentation of the concept of personal boundaries—so important for those whose boundaries have been breached by emotional abuse. This book is the first, but there are many more in the Boundaries series, specific to different age groups and situations. At The Center, we use and recommend these books on a regular basis.

Ellis, Albert, PhD, and Marcia Grad Powers. *The Secret to Overcoming Verbal Abuse: Getting Off the Emotional Roller Coaster and Regaining Control of Your Life* (Wilshire Book Company, 2000). So much of emotional abuse comes through the spoken word. This invaluable book takes you step by step through freeing yourself from the chains of a verbally abusive person and finding your dignity and personal power.

Engel, Beverly, MFCC. *The Emotionally Abused Woman: Overcoming Destructive Patterns and Reclaiming Yourself* (Ballantine Books, 1990). This book is written from the point of view of a marriage, family, and child therapist, and from a woman who has experienced these issues firsthand.

Evans, Patricia. *The Verbally Abusive Relationship*, second edition (Adams Media, 1996). This book looks at the damaging effects of verbal abuse on children and the family. It is written for those suffering from verbal abuse and for therapists treating those with verbal abuse issues. It is especially strong in outlining the different categories of verbal abuse.

Farmer, Steven, MA, MFCC. *Adult Children of Abusive Parents: A Healing Program for Those Who Have Been Physically, Sexually, or Emotionally Abused* (Ballantine Books, 1990). This book offers an insightful presentation on the adult effects of childhood emotional abuse. It includes a program for grieving your lost childhood, becoming your own parent, and experiencing recovery in your adult life.

Forward, Dr. Susan, with Craig Buck. *Toxic Parents: Overcoming Their Hurtful Legacy and Reclaiming Your Life* (Bantam Books, 1990). This book is written to be used by adults who desire to free themselves from the frustrating patterns of their relationship with their abusive parents. The author uses numerous examples of real people to show readers how to develop confidence, strength, and emotional independence.

Garbarino, James, PhD, and Ellen deLara, PhD. *And Words Can Hurt Forever: How to Protect Adolescents from Bullying, Harassment, and Emotional Violence* (The Free Press, 2002). The home is not the only environment in which emotional abuse takes place. This book alerts parents and others to the dangers of an emotionally abusive school environment.

Hirigoyen, Marie-France. *Stalking the Soul: Emotional Abuse and the Erosion of Identity* (Helen Marks Books, 2000). This book, translated from the original French, presents an analysis of the manipulative patterns present in destructive relationships.

Ketterman, Dr. Grace. *Verbal Abuse: Healing the Hidden Wound* (Vine Books, 1993). This book looks at the types of family systems that perpetuate verbal abuse, as well as those most at risk for being abused and for verbally abusing others.

Miller, Alice. *The Truth Will Set You Free: Overcoming Emotional Blindness and Finding Your True Adult Self* (Basic Books, 2001). The author of *The Drama of the Gifted Child*, Miller looks at the dangers to the adult self of ignoring childhood pain. This book includes an important section on recent research on brain development and the effects of trauma.

Miller, Mary Susan, PhD. *No Visible Wounds: Identifying Nonphysical Abuse of Women by Their Men* (Ballantine Books, 1995). Dr. Miller presents a stark picture of the ways women are abused in relationships and offers guidelines on how to leave an abusive relationship.

Palatnik, Lori, with Bob Burg. *Gossip: Ten Pathways to Eliminate It from Your Life and Transform Your Soul* (Simcha Press, 2002). Emotional abuse takes many different forms. Some of the most damaging words to a person's sense of self and to relationships come in the form of gossip. Harmless? Hardly—this book tells you why.

Sarno, John E., MD. *The Mindbody Prescription: Healing the Body, Healing the Pain* (Warner Books, 1998). Dr. Sarno makes a compelling case for the link between emotional trauma and physical pain. His book presents information on a variety of physical symptoms, including gastrointestinal disorders, circulatory problems, headache, allergies, fibromyalgia, infections, chronic fatigue syndrome, and hives.

Related Books by Dr. Jantz

God Can Help You Heal (Publications International, 2007). This simple little book shows you how truth, acceptance, forgiveness, and gratitude can lead to transformation, spiritual intimacy, connection, and vision. It is a devotional book on how to find true healing in your life.

Hope, Help, and Healing for Eating Disorders (Shaw, 2002). Much eating disorder behavior stems from emotional abuse and family issues. This newly expanded and revised edition presents the whole-person approach to healing from eating disorders, including anorexia, bulimia, and compulsive overeating.

How to De-Stress Your Life (Spire, 2008). This book is for anyone who has experienced physical, emotional, and spiritual burnout due to damaging patterns of the past, including emotional and verbal abuse.

Moving Beyond Depression (Shaw, 2003). The destructive effects of childhood emotional abuse can manifest in adult depression, even years after the abuse. This book explores a whole-person approach to recovery from depression—and its debilitating physical, emotional, and spiritual effects.

Internet Resources

www.aplaceofhope.com. This is the home page for The Center for Counseling and Health Resources, Inc., founded by Dr. Jantz.

www.caringonline.com. A news, information, and referral website for those suffering from eating disorders. Affiliated with The Center for Counseling and Health Resources, Inc.

http://pcaamerica.channing-bete.com. This is the web address for short, informative booklets on emotional abuse for general audiences, teens, and parents.

Gregory L. Jantz, PhD, is a popular speaker and an award-winning author. He is a certified chemical dependency professional, a licensed mental health counselor, and a nationally certified eating disorder specialist. Dr. Jantz is the founder of The Center for Counseling and Health Resources, Inc., a leading mental health and chemical dependency treatment facility with a treatment center in the Puget Sound region near Seattle, Washington.

The Center for Counseling and Health Resources, Inc., specializes in whole-person care, with individuals from across the United States and around the world coming to participate in the hope-filled work of recovery. Dr. Jantz's whole-person approach addresses the emotional, relational, intellectual, physical, and spiritual dimensions of each person with a unique, tailored treatment plan. Over the past twenty-four years, Dr. Jantz and The Center have treated thousands of people, using the successful whole-person approach for depression, anxiety, eating disorders, trauma, spiritual crises, and relationship issues.

Dr. Jantz's compassionate, solution-oriented viewpoints on timely topics, plus his natural gift for storytelling, make him a sought-after guest on local and national radio and television. He speaks nationally at conferences, seminars, and retreats on a wide variety of topics, utilizing his extensive expertise and experience.

Dr. Jantz has authored numerous bestselling books, including a book used in the treatment of eating disorders, *Hope, Help, and Healing for Eating Disorders*. His other books include *Losing Weight Permanently; The Spiritual Path to Weight Loss; 21 Days to Eating Better; How to De-Stress Your Life; Hidden Dangers of the Internet; Too Close to the Flame: Recognizing and Avoiding Sexualized Relationships; Turning the Tables on Gambling: Hope and Help for an Addictive Behavior; Moving Beyond Depression; God Can Help You Heal; The Molding of a Champion; Healthy Habits, Healthy Kids; Thin Over 40; The Total Temple Makeover*; and *The Body God Designed*.

Dr. Jantz has been married for twenty-four years to his wife, LaFon. They have been blessed with two sons, Gregg and Benjamin.

Ann McMurray is a freelance writer living in Brier, Washington. She has worked with Dr. Jantz on *Healing the Scars of Emotional Abuse; Hope, Help, and Healing for Eating Disorders; Hidden Dangers of the Internet; Too Close to the Flame: Recognizing and Avoiding Sexualized Relationships; Turning the Tables on Gambling: Hope and Help for an Addictive Behavior; Moving Beyond Depression; God Can Help You Heal; The Molding of a Champion; Healthy Habits, Healthy Kids; Thin Over Forty; The Total Temple Makeover*; and *The Body God Designed*.

McMurray's partnership with Dr. Jantz also extends to The Center for Counseling and Health Resources, Inc., where she works as executive assistant.

She has been married to her husband, Tad, for thirty years and has two adult children, Joel and Lindsay.

For more information about resources related to emotional abuse, or to speak to someone, you may call The Center's toll-free number, (888) 771-5166. For more information about The Center or to receive information about additional resources, go to www.aplaceofhope.com, or write to The Center for Counseling and Health Resources, Inc., P.O. Box 700, Edmonds, WA 98020.

YOU CAN LIVE FREE FROM ANXIETY

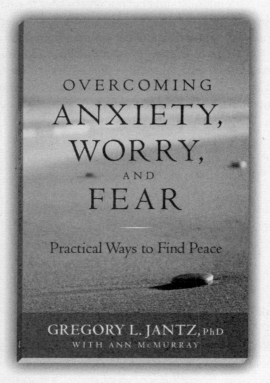

With compassion, common sense, and biblical wisdom, Dr. Jantz will help you identify the causes of your anxiety, assess the severity of your symptoms, and start down avenues for positive change.